SUCCESSFUL PARENTING FOR STRESSFUL TIMES

DENNIS LEES, Ph.D.

Published by
R & E Publishers
P. O. Box 2008
Saratoga, California 95070

Library of Congress Card Catalog Number
85-061381

I.S.B.N.
0-88247-744-7

Library of Congress Cataloging-in-Publication Data

Lees, Dennis, 1939–
    Successful parenting for stressful times.

    Bibliography: p.
    1. Parenting—United States. 2. Child rearing—
United States. 3. Child psychology. I. Title.
HQ755.8.L435 1985   649'.1   85–61381
ISBN 0-88247-744-7

THIS BOOK IS DEDICATED TO:

*My own parents, for their love, example, and
continuing friendship;*

*My children, now grown, for turning out to be
such a source of pride and joy;*

*My wife, for being my best friend, and an out-
standing parent and stepparent.*

TABLE OF CONTENTS

ACKNOWLEDGEMENTS. vii

INTRODUCTION. ix

SECTION I   PUTTING YOURSELF FIRST SHOWS
YOU CARE

    CHAPTER 1   AVOIDING BURNOUT 3
        A Priority For Parents

    CHAPTER 2   "HEALTHY SELFISHNESS" IS A BETTER
IDEA. 9
        You Owe It To The Ones You Love

    CHAPTER 3   ON THE ROAD TO A HAPPIER LIFE. 17
        Eight Steps To Get You On Your Way

SECTION II   THE "BIG THREE" YOU NEED TO KNOW
AS A PARENT

    CHAPTER 4   COMMUNICATION 29
        The Foundation Of A Good Relationship

    CHAPTER 5   SELF-IMAGE AND SELF-ESTEEM 39
        How To Build Them Up

    CHAPTER 6   RULES AND DISCIPLINE 47
        Authoritative vs Authoritarian

SECTION III   DESERVING OF SPECIAL ATTENTION

CHAPTER 7   SINGLE PARENTS. 61
The Toughest Job

CHAPTER 8   STEPPARENTING 69
A Little Different Challenge

CHAPTER 9   LIVING WITH YOUR TEENAGER 77
Understanding Them And You

SECTION IV   THERE'S STILL TIME

CHAPTER 10   THE MOST IMPORTANT ADVICE
FOR PARENTS 87
Remember To. . .

ADDENDUM Some Reading Suggestions 89

ACKNOWLEDGEMENTS

Special thanks to my colleagues at Walnut Creek Counseling Associates for their positive influences on my professional life, for their many useful suggestions regarding this book, and for being among my closest personal friends: Bob Wilk, Jan Howard, Nancy Bascom and Julie Blunden.

Thanks to my clients over the years, my greatest teachers, for supplying the challenges that inspired me to think, research, and re-think my therapeutic policies and practices to a point that I feel I have something to say in a book like this.

Many special thanks to my four children and stepchildren who have enriched my life so much (and also supplied some of the challenges that made this book possible); and to my parents for the foundation based on love which I received from them.

Finally, I owe a large debt of gratitude to my copy editor, Kathleen Mulroy, for her invaluable contributions to this work; and especially to my wife, Judy, my favorite unpaid consultant and most valued confidant.

INTRODUCTION

As I write this, the 1984 United States presidential primaries are just over and the campaign is beginning in earnest. We have been hearing a lot about who is best qualified for "the toughest job in the world" — meaning the U. S. presidency.

I'd like to suggest that no presidential candidate is seeking the toughest job in the world, or the most important. That job already belongs to the millions of people called parents.

The purpose of this book is to share some ideas and observations from my years of experience as both a parent and a family therapist. I hope this will help other parents raise their children more successfully and enjoyably. I believe that parents usually do the best they can; but there is always some room for improvement. New information, inspiration, or even problems can spur us on to seek a better life.

Successful Parenting For Stressful Times is the result of my years of teaching, consulting and counseling on parental stress, school, child development and family and parenting issues. A primary reason I decided to write this book is that I hope to reach a wider audience. I hope to give people additional resources for problem-solving and personal growth. This can help parents to view themselves as "resident experts" and feel less insecure and worried about their task as parents.

A point I hope to make throughout this book is that each of us has more power to direct our life than we are usually aware of. I believe that the more parents develop their abilities to handle their lives and family situations well, the happier they will feel. Also, they will approach problems—which they might otherwise depend on outside experts to solve—more confidently.

I'd like more people to give themselves credit for being good parents. I'd like parents to become aware of their successes and positive experiences in contributing to their children's growth and development.

In summary, this book is an effort to help parents develop more appreciation of themselves, fine-tune their parenting techniques and increase their feelings of confidence and satisfaction in the job they are doing.

The first part of the book is focused on the parent as a person who needs to take the best possible care of him- or herself. (For purposes of simplicity, the word "he" is used throughout to denote both male and female.) I strongly believe that if a parent does not take good care of himself he cannot take the best care of others.

The second part of the book discusses the three most basic things a parent needs to understand, then integrate skillfully into his parenting practices: communication; self-image/self-esteem; and rules and discipline.

The third part is devoted to three categories of parents with unique situations who deserve special mention and attention: single parents; stepparents; and parents of teens. As a former single parent, current stepparent, and parent of teenagers (now grown), I feel particularly close to people dealing with the demands of these situations.

Finally, the closing chapter sums up my view of parents as people and is intended to be a two-page handbook and refresher course. Because of my strong belief in the value of reading material as a resource, a rather extensive booklist is offered at the end of this book for those wishing to pursue more information for themselves and their children.

This book is intended to be a wide-ranging guidebook rather than an exhaustive study of one subject. It is not intended to discuss or attempt to solve *all* problems a parent might encounter but rather to clarify basic premises, offer guidelines and help parents look at their own philosophy and practices. I hope it will be useful to people who are seeking to accomplish, to the best of their ability, a task which is at times difficult but is potentially very rewarding.

My best wishes to you who have taken on "the toughest job in the world."

SECTION I
PUTTING YOURSELF FIRST
SHOWS YOU CARE

CHAPTER 1
AVOIDING BURNOUT
A Priority For Parents

"Are you kidding? I hardly have time *now* for all the things I have to do. How in the world am I going to find time for more?" It was uncharacteristic of Joanne to be angry, outspoken and impatient. Yet this was her response to my comment that she needed to do something for herself, or she was likely to become more unhappy and dissatisfied than she was already.

I knew she was a very good parent, and a person who would gladly help out a neighbor or someone else who needed her, if she could. She tried to find time to help with a school project if asked, listened to her children's fears, complaints and successes whenever possible, and worked hard to keep the house looking nice even when she was tired from working all day.

As I listened to Joanne, I felt both sad and frustrated because I knew she was headed for trouble—big trouble. It became clear as we talked that at this time I was not going to be able to convince her that she needed to consider some changes in her life, and her family's life, or her problems would worsen.

Several weeks later, Joanne was sitting in my office, sobbing uncontrollably, looking exhausted. "But I love my kids," she insisted. "Why am I so moody and impatient lately? I've never felt this way before—it's not like me."

She went on to tell how she had been needlessly hard on the children and her husband in recent weeks. Carl was a good father and husband whose only real fault seemed to be that he was gone long hours, commuting and at his job, and was not quite as available to help out as Joanne would like. "I've been im-

"

possible to live with for weeks now, and for no good reason," she said.

I stopped her there. "No good reason?" In fact, there was a very good reason for what was happening. Joanne was worn out, drained, a victim of what is commonly referred to these days as "burnout."

Burnout doesn't usually happen to people who have serious emotional problems or are easily frustrated. In fact, it tends to occur in people who are generally healthy, hardworking and caring, people who want the best for others and are willing to give of themselves whenever possible.

As a family therapist in a large, solidly middle-class suburban area, I've become increasingly concerned about the growing number of people I see and hear about who are feeling under stress, tired and wondering if being a parent is worth it. That is not a difficult viewpoint to understand, considering how complex and demanding life can be, with the pressures of careers, financial problems, schoolwork and other concerns about one's children, and keeping a marriage or one's personal life healthy.

Burnout doesn't occur overnight. It is more likely to be a slow-to-develop condition which occurs for a variety of reasons. It may actually be a good thing for some people, because it can force them to look at issues of potential problem areas in their lives that otherwise they would continue to avoid. If a person realizes that he or she is under too much unhealthy stress, he may be forced to re-set priorities or make lifestyle changes that are long overdue. In this way we might say burnout is the best thing that could happen.

However, while one is experiencing it, burnout does not seem a positive condition. In fact, it can be downright dangerous and it is certainly unwise to ignore it.

So, how do you know when burnout is happening to you? You probably won't have much trouble realizing it, if you are reasonably aware and honest with yourself. What has come to be known as burnout is essentially a state of emotional or physical exhaustion. You feel depleted and drained, and perhaps resentful that you have given but not received much in return. Often physical tiredness, emotional irritability, indifference, detachment, or feeling that you are unappreciated are early signs of burnout. Other factors in feeling out of sorts may include recent lack of rest, ill health, or a setback in an otherwise satisfying life; these situations can aggravate a developing case of burnout.

If you are experiencing two or more of the above symptoms, you are getting a message that all is not well. There are three books in the section on suggested readings at the back of this book which you may wish to refer to for detailed explanations and information on how and why burnout occurs.

I believe the key factors in a progression toward burnout are:

- Experiencing a lack of balance in life, especially balance between emotional "in-come and out-go," resulting in basic needs being unmet.

- Holding idealized rather than realistic images of how life should be, creating frequent frustration.

- Having too-high or unrealistic expectations of oneself or others; in other words, being a perfectionist.

- Feeling a lack of satisfaction, powerlessness, meaninglessness, which drain off the sense of fulfillment necessary to make life seem worthwhile.

- Finally, experiencing fatigue, boredom, resentment, emptiness as you feel more and more unnurtured. At this stage you feel that nobody cares and neither do you.

In the working world, workaholics are often prime candidates for burnout. These people may look like very effective and productive workers, but in the long run they are barely average in effectiveness and productivity. They look good and reach their peak quickly but may burn out soon if not given a constant supply of invigorating new challenges to keep them going. What often happens is that the workaholic feels the need to make a very good impression and is willing to pay almost any price to do so. Another possibility is that he may be focusing so much on work as a way to avoid personal problems or family relationship difficulties. A boss may admire a workaholic, but this behavior pattern is not good for the person or the family involved, in terms of long-term happiness.

Of course, being narrowly focused and devoted to one

thing is sometimes necessary for a defined period of time, such as when one is finishing college, writing a book, or starting a new job. However, if this is done for a long time or if the person is unaware of possible harmful effects of this lifestyle, it can be very unhealthy. A workaholic is likely to forget about, or try to ignore, the multiple needs we all have and may be well on the road to burning out without realizing it.

The workaholic's situation is similar to what can happen to a parent who allows his out-of-balance life to continue without corrective measures being taken. Such a person is likely to have problems, such as excessive drinking. This may be his response to family, marital or health problems or an inability or unwillingness to get along with others; or it may be the only way he knows to relax or feel a sense of relief from pressure.

Frequently, the truly productive, dependable worker has been shown to be a person who has a well-rounded life. This usually means a person has important things outside of his job that give meaning and fill time, such as belief and activity in a cause or religion; strong family or friendship ties; a hobby or involvement in sports. These things refresh, nourish and help maintain one's perspective.

Some of the situations that get in the way of being a better parent, and which tend to produce burnout, are doing too much, trying too hard, and being "spread too thin." As for the workaholic, unrealistic standards and a lack of balance contribute to the development of burnout. The burned out parent is often one who is prone to feeling guilty if he doesn't believe he is doing enough or doing his very best. This parent may have a lot of variety and activity in his life but not enough satisfaction. A guilty person finds it very hard to feel satisfied and peaceful—he never does quite enough, never fully proves he is a good person. When faced with even normal hurdles in life, this person tends to react in ways that make sense on the surface but actually contribute to his problems.

A few years ago I cut out of a newspaper a letter to Dr. Joyce Brothers which illustrates what can happen to a parent—or anyone in a demanding situation—when resources run out before responsibilities do. (Since I didn't note the date of her column, I can't give proper credit, but I hope she won't mind if I share her column.)

"Dear Dr. Brothers: I know the children's teen years are hard on parents, but I never thought they'd be this hard. My husband and I are at the point where we think we've had it! How much should a parent be asked to give? We've tried to understand, we've been loving, loving and more loving and now, I'm sick of the role of parent, I'm bitter and it's beyond my comprehension why anyone would elect to become a parent. I regret to say I don't really like my children anymore. I think they're intolerably selfish and self-centered. There, I've said it! Now what on earth can I do about it? I can't simply kick them out on the street. I can't turn them in and exchange them for sweet, sensitive, loving human beings. I'm stuck. —B.N.''

Dr. Brothers' response was to note that this mother is not alone in her feelings and that parents who care about their children are prime candidates for parental burnout. Of course, some parents may benefit from individual, couple or family counseling to help them cope with the intense strain they are feeling. But let's first look at other ideas that may help people like the above mother.

CHAPTER 2
"HEALTHY SELFISHNESS"
IS A BETTER IDEA
You Owe It To The Ones You Love

Mark and Sarah J. wearily told me, during a marriage counseling session, about the decline in their relationship during the past few years. The noticeable decline began about the time their two children, Mark, Jr., and Kathy, approached adolescence. It seemed that no matter what they did for the kids, Mark and Sarah felt unappreciated. Also, they were frustrated at a lack of closeness both between them and with the children.

Mark and Sarah both work and are gone from home long hours, but they love their children very much and are willing to make sacrifices for their happiness. Three years ago they bought a large, comfortable home in one of the best areas of their suburban community. The beautifully landscaped backyard boasts a swimming pool and half of the garage is taken up by Mark, Jr.'s pool table.

Mark said to me, "We've tried to give the children everything they need or want, but still they don't seem appreciative and don't like to spend much time with us. They prefer their teenage friends instead."

Mark and Sarah's solution has been to try harder, to expect more and more of themselves and their children, to plan family outings whenver possible and spend a little more money than they can afford on stereos, ski trips and clothes for Mark, Jr. and Kathy. As a result, Mark and Sarah spend less time and money on themselves and are feeling it is all futile. They have a growing, gnawing feeling that emptiness is creeping into their once-happy family life.

What's the answer? Are they bad parents? Are the children slipping away and headed for trouble? Will they be tempted by drugs or become school dropouts? Is family life, as they knew it, a thing of the past? Should they read some books or get counseling?

Let's take a closer look at what's happening. Mark and Sarah have given up a lot for their children. That, in itself, is not bad; parents should give to their children, even sacrifice for them when necessary. But has this couple given too much, more than they could really afford emotionally, without replenishing their own resources? Perhaps they are trying too hard to be perfect.

I have a saying I asked Mark and Sarah to remember: "You can't give out of an empty basket." No matter how much you want to give, or someone needs you to give, if your basket is empty , you can't give out of it. But the answer is not to stop giving; it is to be sure to keep your basket filled so you *can* give.

Burnout can occur in anyone's life and doesn't have to be in an advanced stage to be a serious concern and in need of attention. As in the practice of physical medicine, the best treatment is prevention whenever possible. You should be aware of the developing problem and catch it in the early stages.

The good news is that most burnout conditions can be treated and improved, even in advanced stages.

When counseling people like Mark and Sarah J., I ask them to think about a concept I developed during the past few years, "Healthy Selfishness," and how it might apply to their lives. Before defining this concept and discussing how to put it into practice, I want to note a couple of principles involved in burnout. The single most important thing to remember about its causes, cure or prevention is that you must be willing to acknowledge a problem exists.

In other words, you must take responsibility for yourself and your own well-being. In so doing, you are also accepting responsibility for the secondary well-being of those who depend on you for care or other needs. This acceptance of responsibility also implies a wish to get better, to develop more satisfactory living habits and to see that one's needs are met.

The other principle, and the point I want to make before discussing healthy selfishness in more detail, is the notion of balance. Without balance in our lives, we invite trouble. I believe our world is an excellent example of this point. If our planet were closer to the sun it would burn up, whereas if it were any further away from the sun it would freeze. As it is, we are in perfect balance with, and receive life-support from, the sun because the earth is balanced in our universe. In the physical realm, the necessity for both exercise and rest for the health of our bodies is another illustration of balance.

Now, assuming you have decided you want to prevent or cure burnout, what do you do? Frist, you must realize your need to clarify how and why burnout is happening to you, be willing to work on necessary changes, and understand the importance of responsibility and balance as basic factors.

Next, you should understand "Healthy Selfishness." It is a simple concept, with three principles and three steps. The principles are:

- Learning to be more self-nurturing;

- Getting what you need from others;

- Continuing to meet your responsibilities to others who depend on you, such as children, spouse, employer, friends.

The three steps to take are to:

- Discover how you feel about your life now;

- Identify what is working well and what is missing in your life;

- Devise a plan for rebuilding satisfaction back into your life, replenishing resources on a regular basis, and accomplishing whatever else is needed for your well-being.

You may be surprised when you take these steps, especially if you're really honest with yourself. Some people find that a complete restructuring of their lives is called for, involving major changes such as a new job or career, a move to a new area, or a change in lifestyle or goals. Usually, though, people decide on more subtle adjustments such as finding more time to relax and play, seeking new hobbies or friends, or learning new skills that will enrich their lives. For everyone these changes are likely to mean more personal satisfaction and better relationships with the "important others" in life, such as family members, friends and co-workers.

To help you get started in your self-evaluation, I have devised a short "quiz" which you can take in ten or fifteen minutes. Remember, this is your personal survey—you don't have to share the results with anyone unless you want to. It is usually best to put down your first thought in response to each item since this is usually the most accurate response. There are no right or wrong answers since all you are seeking is some insight into your feelings and thoughts as a guide to developing a plan for healthy selfishness that will work for you.

1. On a scale of 1 to 10, I rate my overall life now: _________
2. On a scale of 1 to 10, I rate my personal life now: ________
3. On a scale of 1 to 10, I rate my job-related life now: ______
4. What I like most about my personal life currently is: ______

   ____
5. What I dislike most about my personal life currently is:

   ____
6. What I like most about my job-related life currently is:

   ____
7. What I dislike most about my job-related life currently is:

   ____
8. Things I enjoy doing on a regular basis include: _________

   ____
9. What can really interest or excite me more than anything else is: ____
10. What seems to be missing in my life is: _______________

   ____
11. Things I feel guilty or uneasy about include: ___________

   ____
12. I experience the greatest stress in my life when: _________

   ____
13. If I could change two or three things in the near future they would be: ____
14. My greatest satisfactions in life come from: ____________

   ____
15. What I need from "important others" in my life is: _______

   ____
16. The best way for me to relax is: ____________________

   ____
17. What I could do to take better care of myself is: _________

   ____

18. Some reasons I don't seem to take better care of myself are:
____

19. If I were to practice healthy selfishness (nurturing myself and others while also meeting my responsibilities), this would mean doing these things: _______________
____

20. Priorities I need to establish in my life are (number from 1 on, in order of their importance): _______________
____
____

Do you feel guilty about focusing on your needs? I hope not. Remember that everyone benefits—you, your children and anyone else who depends on you—when you are happier and more satisfied. In other words, everyone wins when you win. Children don't win when parents lose, and, of course, parents don't win if it is at the unreasonable expense of their children.

The next step in attempting to meet your needs is to do a more detailed self-evaluation. I'd like you to take a few minutes to make three lists relating to goals for you and your children. Most people think, "I shouldn't make goals for my kids—that's their job," but in fact most of us do have some wishes or goals for our children, so you may as well be honest with yourself. These three lists can be long or short, as general or specific as you wish. One caution: don't leave off something because you think it's not important enough or it is too far-fetched or too long-range. Put down anything that comes to mind.

I. GOALS FOR MYSELF (personal, job-related, hobbies, etc.)

II.   GOALS REGARDING RELATIONSHIPS (friends, spouse,
        co-workers, children, etc.)

III.   GOALS REGARDING CHILDREN

Now, go back and note in the margin your number one priority in each of these three categories, then, in order of importance, the rest of your goals in each category. The purpose of this is simply to help you clarify what feels important to you now, which things might be most in need of your attention, what might be most worth pursuing for your greatest happiness and satisfaction.

Finally, here are some sentence completion exercises.

1.   As a person, what matters most to me is __________________

____

2.   As a parent, what matters most to me is __________________

____

3.   What I seem to need is _________________________________

____

4.   My long-range dreams include ___________________________

____

5.   Ways I keep myself from achieving happiness include ______

____

6.   I want or need from others _____________________________

____

7.   What might keep me from meeting my responsibilities to others who depend on me is ________________________________

____

8.   I have recently learned about myself that ________________

____

9.   I plan to ____

____

CHAPTER 3
ON THE ROAD TO A HAPPIER LIFE
Eight Steps To Get You On Your Way

Parents have the most difficult, responsible and potentially satisfying job in the world. I strongly encourage you to give yourself credit for the complexity of the tasks facing you rather than down-playing your job as a parent and perhaps kidding yourself that all will be well without paying careful attention to how it's going for you as well as for your children. On the other hand, I also encourage you not to try so hard and worry so much that you drain off energy that could be used to deal effectively with your family's life as it unfolds.

In this chapter we will look at some things you can do to enrich your life and thereby improve the job you can do as a parent. It is this constant replenishing of resources that can "keep your basket full" so you can be the kind of parent you really want to be.

1. Become as clear as you can about your needs, goals, alternatives, what works or doesn't work for you. In other words, become as familiar as you can with what makes you happy, where you want to head in your life, what resources you presently have, and so on. Don't forget also to consider what you don't have now, but would like to have, noting resources you could develop and realistic possibilities that exist for you, even if they may not happen immediately. You have already done much of this step in the quiz and exercises in Chapter 2. However, this is a step to be taken periodically, to reevaluate and check up on yourself, to see how you are doing and what fine-tuning or refocusing might be needed.

2. **Notice all there is to like** and be happy about in your life. Be willing to have a positive outlook about yourself and life in general. This simple step, or point of view, can work miracles because it helps to keep you oriented to positives and possibilities rather than to negatives and problems. As you do this, be sure to notice what you are willing to give yourself credit for, what is already good, satisfying, or at least acceptable. This includes recognizing and coming to terms with whatever weaknesses or faults you think you have. Notice anything you would like to change without berating yourself for being less than perfect. A famous psychologist once said, "Perfectionism is a curse." He was right.

3. **Take time to play in your life.** Here are some suggestions on how to get started:

- *Develop your sense of humor.* Go to a funny movie, read the comics in the newspaper before reading anything else, look for the lighter side or ironic, ridiculous situations in the news. Learn to laugh rather than get mad at yourself when you make a mistake; try telling someone about it, if you can do so without being taken seriously or criticized. If you have a favorite comedian or entertainer, go to one of their shows in person. Buy a paperback book of cartoons and read some before going to sleep at night; end your day with a smile. In other words, do something to lighten your day and your point of view, and increase your willingness to smile. Remember that happiness is much more a chosen point of view than the result of circumstances.

- *Plan ahead for an occasional evening, day or weekend away.* Even a simple thing like meeting a friend for lunch or an after-work drink can be a welcome and refreshing break in your routine, and a nice thing to look forward to. An evening at a play or concert, a museum opening or other community event affords an opportunity to meet new people or to open yourself to new kinds of experiences and interests.

- *Take a class or get active in an organization or cause you believe in.* Get involved! Explore some activity or group you have been curious about for a while but never got around to looking into. Do something you have been putting off or "didn't have time for." Finding and participating in things that have meaning can be exhilarating and energizing.

- *Have a "just for fun" day.* Why not take the children out for a soda or ice cream on a Saturday afternoon? Or spend a whole evening or weekend loafing and not feeling guilty about it. There doesn't have to be a reason for everything we do. "Just for fun" is sometimes reason enough.

- *Create an adventure of some kind.* Use your imagination! What would be fun, or exciting, or different?

- *Go to a travel agency and gather some brochures to plan your dream vacation(s).* Maybe you could take a short, inexpensive vacation next year, and plan an all-time, long-wished-for Big Vacation to be taken in several years. Start saving a little each week toward your trips; actually set some goals, take them seriously and make it happen.

- *Send the children to a matinee with money for popcorn.* Then make love in the afternoon while they're gone, or do whatever else appeals to you.

- *Odds and ends.* Compliment someone on something they did well or on their new outfit. Rent a limousine or fancy sedan for a special event or evening on the town. Read a book from the best-seller list and share it with a friend. Take a bike ride or a hike. Learn to play a new sport or an instrument. Buy a new album or tape each week or month and create the time to listen to it.

4. **Learn to use stress reduction techniques as a means of relaxing or recharging.** We all need to develop ways to escape from pressures but can't always take a week or weekend in the mountains, or even a day on the golf course. More routine, less time-consuming ways, therefore, need to be found which we can include in our daily lives. Here are some ways you may find helpful:

- *Notice your breathing.* Is it deep or shallow? Fast and anxious, or slow and relaxed? Unless you're being chased by a large bear, or have just be chewed out by the boss, your breathing should be fairly deep, slow and relaxed. If not, you're probably more tense than you should be and should pay attention to your pulse rate and breathing habits. It may sound over-simplified, but the truth is that paying attention to breathing is one of the easiest and most effective ways to monitor and control tension and stress. Take a moment now to notice your breathing. If it is shallow, fast, or seems to be more in your upper chest or throat, you are probably not breathing as efficiently as you could. Proper breathing is, in itself, calming and is very easy to learn. Once learned and incorporated as a habit, it will naturally take the place of shallow, inefficient breathing.

    In less than ten minutes you can assess and, if necessary, begin to change your breathing habits. Find a time and place where you can sit quietly and comfortably, preferably in a chair that allows you to sit up straight, even stretch up just a little, to allow for full air flow. (1) Focus on the *pace* of your breathing, notice if it is fast or slow. (2) Next, focus on the *location*—where do you breathe from? Is it from your diaphragm or belly area, or from your upper chest and throat? Now, after noticing the pace and location of your breathing, start breathing slower, slower, slower, until it feels natural. If you try too hard, you could become more tense instead of less, so just do it calmly. Second, start breathing more deeply, from the abdominal area. Draw air into the area behind your navel, allowing it to calmly, slowly, fully fill up your upper body area. Once you've got the pace and location of your breathing identified and have practiced each, paying attention as you do so, put them together. Practice quietly, calmly breathing slowly and deeply. If you develop this two-step practice as a regular, habitual part of your life, it will likely come naturally very soon. You will be meeting your body's needs for a more calmly paced intake of fresh air and fuller release of "used" air with the result of feeling more relaxed. Air is free, so claim and fully use your fair share!

- *Close your eyes and take a journey through your body.* This is an especially useful exercise at times when you feel tension mounting, but is also useful as a regular, daily exercise to prevent tension build-up. As you travel through your body, notice where you hold or are building up tension. Start at either the top of your head or at your toes, which I prefer, and work your way to the other end, like this: As you sit quietly, eyes closed, start with your toes, up through your feet, legs, pelvic area, chest, back, arms, neck, face and scalp, simply noticing any feeling of tension or stress in any of those areas. Are there any tight spots, aches, muscle soreness or tingling sensations? Now, go back to those tension sites and calmly decide to release the tension there, one spot at a time. If you have several tension sites you may find it best to concentrate on one at a time and only go on to others as you feel tension lessening. If deciding to let go of tension doesn't seem to work, don't worry. Keep at it, knowing that practice and more familiarity with the process will bring results soon.

Another approach to releasing tension is this: Picture yourself "breathing to" a tension site. Breathing to, or breathing into, a particular spot means focusing your attention on one area as you breathe in fresh air, allowing your attention and the air to have a soothing, healing effect. Allow yourself to be calmed as you breathe to a tension site.

Still another way to release tension is to physically discharge it. Basically what you do to accomplish this is to tense or flex, then release each muscle, muscle group or tension site. You can also breathe in as you tense and breathe out as you release. (Again, as you do this exercise, allow yourself to release the tension, to be calmed and to benefit from the exercise. If you don't think you can relax anyway, or don't think anything can help, you'll probably prove yourself to be right.) Here's how you might proceed with tensing/flexing, then releasing while breathing: With eyes, lips, jaw, etc., clench while inhaling, then release while exhaling. With the neck area as your focus, push the head forward, backward, then roll it to each side while inhaling then exhaling. With the arms and legs, flex-release then stretch/release, and so on. As you practice and become familiar with the exercise process, you will probably find it to be more effective and easier to do.

Other methods of releasing body tension may work as well or better for you, such as meditation or exercise. Biofeedback is one of the newer, often very effective tools for learning stress reduction. The technique involves tuning into one's subconscious mind through deep relaxation. Biofeedback usually involves not only breathing and meditation techniques, but also evaluates the function of exercise, diet and lifestyle changes in one's life.

- *Find a quiet place and sit and listen to the stillness.* Reflect on the pleasures that can come from relaxation and quiet, from doing nothing, even if only for a few minutes. Becoming comfortable with solitude and stillness can be remarkably calming, both to the body and to the spirit. It can bring a sense of satisfaction that is deeply replenishing.

- *Take a walk.* A brisk walk in pleasant surroundings can be a means of burning off nervous energy or an opportunity for reflection and deep thought. A slow walk may give you a chance to notice things along the way that you have missed, even if you have been there a hundred times. If you prefer, take along someone you care about and walk quietly together. Or talk about nothing in particular, or take a few minutes to share something that's on your mind.

5. **Realize the great importance of friends and loved ones.** Cultivate friendships that will enrich you and them. Health professionals have known for a long time that satisfying relationships with family and friends are among the best indicators, and most necessary ingredients, of both emotional and physical health. Invest as much as you can in opportunities for friendships or closer family ties. This could obviously include your spouse, children, parents, or grandparents. Not so obviously, you could reach out to next-door neighbors, former classmates, someone at work you'd like to know better. Consider making friends with members of organizations you've thought of joining, with the people around the corner who have waved as you go by, or with parents of your child's classmates you may meet at an open house at school.

I can't stress strongly enough the importance of human relationships to emotional health. When relationships are working well they are a great boon to us, and when they don't exist or aren't going well, we can suffer and miss them greatly. Allow time and energy for this important area of normal human need and potential satisfaction.

6. **Learn the skills of communication.** This is the founda-

tion of a good relationsip. I tell clients in therapy and people in my seminars that "communication is to a relationship as a foundation is to a house." A weak or damaged foundation can make an otherwise beautiful house dangerously unsteady. You don't have to be a great orator who can move large audiences to tears or laughter to be a good communicator. The main ingredient is a willingness to share yourself, your feelings and thoughts, and to be receptive to those of others. It involves some risk-taking and reaching out, and the possibility that you might be hurt or disappointed; but then, you might not. You might even be pleased at the difference good communication can make in the richness of your life and your relationships. In another chapter of this book, communication is explored in depth and I'll give some tips on why and how to do it better.

7. Develop your own "personal affirmations" and "visualizations." These are two simple, effective ways you can put your goals or wishes into action. The point of each is to work toward changing your reality, or the things happening in your life, by picturing feelings or events as you want them to be.

For a successful outcome from these two techniques, (1) your point of view needs to be such that you are ready and willing to accept things the way they are *or* to change them into what you want them to be, and (2) in expressing your affirmations or visualizations, be as specific as possible; it's hard to go after something vague.

Let's talk about each of these concepts. I would define personal affirmations as *statements which are true about you and the intentions you have for your life.* So an affirmation might be either a statement about your life now or your life as you'd like it to be. For instance, you might have as a current personal affirmation the statement that "being a good parent is important to me." Another example, regarding a long-range goal, might be the statement that "I want to become closer and more loving to my wife and children." This statement of clear intention is a goal or wish affirming the person you'd like to become. An example of an affirmation that is a sort of "policy statement" about how you would like to be is: "I will love myself as much as I can at any given time, even when I make mistakes." Other affirmations are: "I really love my kids"; "I am willing to accept life as it comes and be as happy as I can"; "I intend to read at least one good book each month to enrich my life"; "It is okay with me if people are not perfect"; "It is important to me to do my best in everything I do"; "Perfection is not as important to me as enjoying what I'm doing each day". Perhaps in formulating your own personal affirmations, you may want to make two lists, one for you as a parent and one for you as a person. Or, you could make one list for the "current you" and one for you and the future.

If you are having trouble thinking of any affirmations for yourself, look back at your self-evaluation quiz and exercises. Think about what you do or don't feel satisfied with in your life now, or look at your goals. When you have several affirmations in mind that you feel good about, write them down and carry them in your wallet to refer to once or twice a day.

Now, what about visualizations? A visualization is not something a fortune-teller sees in a crystal ball. For our purposes, the definition of a visualization is simply *picturing something the way you would like it to be.* It is a kind of daydreaming, but done consciously or for a purpose. It is turning your goals or wishes into reality by imagining them as being real.

How do you do this? Imagine an event the way you want it to happen. Use your imagination; be realistic but not limiting. Be willing to have what you want and deserve, specifically picture it in your mind. Let it jell and mature, and in real life do what you can to make your vision come true.

Visualization is a way of taking charge of your experience, rather than always taking things the way they are created by others or by 'fate." Of course, we can't always make things exactly the way we'd like them to be. Picturing yourself depositing $100,000 into your bank account tomorrow certainly does not guarantee that event will occur. However, thoughtfully imagining yourself as more prosperous, developing the feeling that you deserve to be financially successful, picturing yourself receiving payment for a product or service you produced, or thinking of yourself as being successful in a business you've long wanted to start are not unrealistic uses of visualization.

8.   Finally, take responsibility for your life, your problems, your potential, and your dreams. Be willing to experience things without being "run" by them as a victim. Know that you are essentially in charge of your life and that the important thing is the overall picture, not the short-lived ups and downs in your life. It has been said many times and in many ways that happiness is being able to choose gladly to either live life as it is or to change it if you can, but to be satisfied with the outcome in any case.

Do what you need to do to take care of yourself, knowing

that you have the primary responsibility for this; everyone around you will benefit as well. Learn to give gladly and fully to others without feeling you have lost yourself. Surrendering is giving in by choice, not giving up.

Pay attention to your body, your emotions and their messages about what is good and right for you. The more you do this, the less attention and effort you will have to devote to making your life work out and the more you can just get on with living well. Develop a positive attitude, seeing problems as opportunities instead of barriers. Look at whatever mistakes you've made or imagined you've made as learning experiences, perhaps even as enriching experiences, but never as proof that you're not a good person.

SECTION II
THE "BIG THREE" YOU NEED TO KNOW AS A PARENT

CHAPTER 4
COMMUNICATION
The Foundation Of A Good Relationship

Several studies in recent years have shown some interesting things about communication. One study done in a large corporation indicated that only about *one-half* of what was said between people was really heard and only about *one-half of that* was understood accurately and remembered for any length of time. So, just *one-fourth* of what was communicated between people really got through. Some experts would say that even this is an overly optimistic figure.

Another study showed that most of what is communicated is through body language, less is through tone of voice and even less through words. We often communicate by eye contact—or lack of it—facial expression, tone of voice and inflection, our actions, touch, and other non-verbal means.

Recently, I attended a workshop where Dr. Stephen Glenn, Director of the Family Development Institute of Washington, D.C., spoke. He said research indicates that, typically, the modern American nuclear family spends less than fifteen minutes a day in parent-child communication. Of that, about twelve minutes are spent "taking care of business," discussing use of the car, the menu for dinner, or questions about why someone wasn't home on time. That leaves less than three minutes for constructive or pleasant interaction in an average day.

Perhaps the main point these studies make is that we don't communicate as effectively or as much as we think we do. This brings to mind a clever, and true, statement: "You cannot *not* communicate (in some form or another)." In a relationship of any kind, messages are given out even if you don't speak; you "say" something even if you don't mean to. An unwillingness to communicate directly may reflect problems in your relationship and your intentions regarding it.

In this chapter we will primarily be discussing verbal communication. In following chapters, particularly those on self-esteem and on rules and discipline, we will discuss some of the ways in which other influences such as attitude and non-verbal clues influence communication.

A saying I mentioned in an earlier chapter is worth repeating here: "Communication is to a relationship as a foundation is to a house." Think about this for a moment. If you have an attractive, expensive house, but it is built on a foundation of weak wood and cracked concrete, what you really have is a relatively worthless house. The same is true of a relationship. It may be that it looks good or seems comfortable, but if there is little or ineffective communication between the people involved, then there is probably not a good relationship. The foundation—communication—is not solid.

When you think of what the word relationship means—namely sharing, interacting, being together, caring—isn't it hard to imagine having a good relationship without good communication?

So, what is communication? One answer is that communication is the vehicle through which we connect with another person, the way we share ourselves and send various kinds of messages between ourselves and other people. It is all the ways you tell someone who you are, what you feel, want or need, how much you do or don't want contact and what you think. In short, it is how we get in touch with the essence of one another. It is how we get to know the truth that exists between us and what the experiences of life are like for one another.

Whether we are communicating verbally or non-verbally, we are expressing more than just the facts of a message. Our attitude—how we are feeling about ourselves physically and emotionally *and* how we are feeling about the other person or the situation—will invariably come across. So, something else that is true about communication is that it is important to pay attention to much more than just the words as we either "send" or "receive" messages.

For instance, it is probably not a good idea to try to discuss an important problem with someone if one or the other feels tired, uninterested or distracted. There are too many barriers working against you, and a positive outcome to the discussion is unlikely.

If you feel it is very important to handle a problem at a time like this, you could simply say that something is on your mind and you'd like a few minutes to talk it over as soon as possible. Wise preparation, and seeing that you have the proper environment and timing for communication, can express your intention to have your relationship work as well as possible.

Even seemingly minor considerations can make a difference in the outcome of your efforts to communicate. For instance, trying to talk to a child who is three feet tall while you are towering over him could intimidate the child. It is better for the adult to kneel down or for the two to sit and talk; this equalizes their positions and allows for better eye contact. A similar point is that uncrossed arms and an open posture communicates your willingness to be with someone, to be open and receptive. Little things like these can make a big difference and have subtle but important influences on the outcome of a discussion.

It is tempting to think that communication is something that comes naturally and is easy and routine. In fact, I believe that good communication is more a learned skill than a natural event that occurs whenever people have something to say to each other. Because it is learned, communication skill is something that we can improve, and thereby improve our relationships.

I'd like to explain two models of communication which I call "linear" and "circular." I think these models demonstrate the definition and purpose of communication.

Often, people think they have "communicated" whenever they have thrown out a statement of some kind. For instance, Dad may say to Billy, "Please take out the trash." In *linear* communication, there is no provision for responding to this type of statement, as this illustration shows:

(1)   (2)

DAD ⟶ _________"Please take out the trash."_________ ⟶ BILLY

(End of transaction between them.)

In this example, several important ingredients for successful communication are lacking. First, Dad doesn't know for sure that Billy heard *or* understood the request. Second, Dad doesn't know what Billy's reaction or response is. Third, if Billy does have a response, he doesn't know Dad's reaction to it. In other words, this transaction between Dad and Billy is very incomplete and is, therefore, fertile ground for a misunderstanding.

This linear or one-line model of communication does not

31

allow for interaction—the clarification and feedback/response that is basic to effective communication. A statement that has merely been thrown out—even though it was a clear request by Dad—is not two-way communication.

Let's look at how *circular* communication allows for a very different outcome. (Keep in mind that we are talking here of effective *communication*, not necessarily immediate compliance or agreement.) The following model includes several possible outcomes:

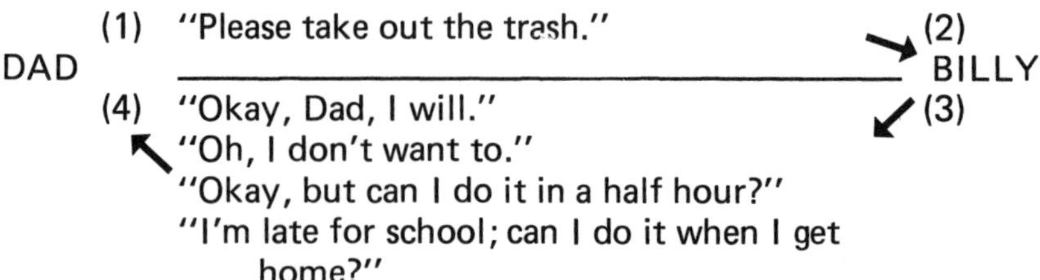

I'll admit it's not likely you will get the first response! But let's assume Billy says, "Okay, but can I do it in a half hour when this T.V. show is over?" And let's also assume Dad then says, "That's fine," and Billy does it then.

A complete transaction has now occurred between them. There was no misunderstanding and the job got done to everyone's satisfaction under the amended agreement, in which they both participated.

To most parents this may seem too good to be true. The circular model does illustrate how effective communication can occur and how each communication "transaction"—a verbal interchange in this case—needs to be complete to be effective. In fact, you could say each transaction is actually a "mini-relationship" in which people are interacting and practicing their relationship.

The complete transaction between Dad and Billy would be illustrated as follows, to include Dad's response:

DAD   "Please take out the trash."   BILLY
         "Okay, but can I do it in a half hour?"
         "Okay, that's fine."

Of course, this circular model does not necessarily mean that Dad will get just what he wants as soon as he makes his request. What it does provide is an opportunity for both parties to deal with whatever comes up when Dad makes his original statement. Each person, in other words, has the same opportunity to say what he wants, how he feels about it and what he agrees to do. If, for some reason, the agreement made is not kept, that will have to be handled in a new transaction between them. However, this would not mean the first transaction had failed. If a broken agreement needs to be dealt with, or a lack of understanding seems to have occurred, you could approach it by saying something like, "What was your understanding of . . . ?" or, "Let me be sure I understand . . ." as a way to clarify and deal with the situation in a non-accusing way.

Again, it is important to remember that good communication does not guarantee compliance or agreement. Communication is a means to interact effectively, express oneself and receive a response.

Sometimes interaction in communication is not for the purpose of solving a problem, such as getting the trash out. It may be that communication is appropriate just to share a feeling or make someone aware of something, such as your political opinions or your plans for the evening.

In any case, the feedback built into this circular method assures that better understanding will likely result.

The next major point regarding the art and craft of good communication is understanding "I-messages," the basic factor in sending appropriate, clear messages.

An I-message is a personal statement that reports your feeling, opinion, demand or request. An I-message might be, "Boy, I sure am (tired, excited, depressed, full of energy, etc.) today." Or, "I really felt upset when I came home and saw the trash wasn't taken out." Or, "I'd like to go out to dinner to-night."

I-messages are not only a way to report or state what you have to say; they are also a means of taking responsibility for what you are saying in a way that's not likely to make the other person feel defensive or otherwise on the spot.

For instance, look at an I—message compared to a "you-message." If you say, "Would you like to go out to dinner?" the other person doesn't know exactly what you are trying to get across. Are you commenting that you want to go out to dinner, suggesting that the two of you go out, or trying to find out if the other person wants to go? If you say, "Why didn't you take out the trash?", are you angry that the trash wasn't taken out or are you trying to make the other person feel guilty?

A you-message is much more likely to convey blame, guilt or criticism, even if that is not your intention. It is also more likely to leave the receiver of your message feeling defensive or cautious, accused or unclear, and, therefore, less able to respond to the real message you intended to get across.

With an I-message, you usually convey more clearly what you intend to say, whether it is a statement, a question or a demand. Then the other person doesn't have to guess or assume—perhaps inaccurately—what you really mean. Because the I-message is also a means of taking responsibility for your statement, by its very structure ("I feel/want/like/think/don't like, etc.") it probably won't leave the other person feeling guilty or defensive.

At the risk of overstating a point, I want to mention again that it is important to remember the purpose of good communication. It is to get people to interact by sharing their feelings and thoughts, so we can know each other and get what we want and need from others. This brings us to another principle regarding good communication—the necessity of understanding that communication is talking *with, not at* the other person.

Thomas Gordon, in his book, *P.E.T. In Action*, illustrates a complete I-message as having three parts. This three-part breakdown is especially useful when you use an I-message to comment on something that bothers you or to discuss a problem.

Here are the three parts of an I-message:
(1) A description of the problem or complaint.
(2) The feeling you are experiencing.
(3) The consequence or effect upon you.

For example, let's say Mom is unhappy about something Jimmy is doing; perhaps arriving home late from his friend's house three blocks away. Her I-message may look like this when it is broken down:
(1) "When you are late coming home from your friend's house
(2) I get worried
(3) because I wonder if something happened to you."

Here Mom is letting Jimmy know exactly what she is feeling as a result of what occurred. She is not accusing him, putting him on the defensive or trying to make him feel guilty. She is simply stating clearly what happened, how she feels and why. She is taking responsibility for her experience—feeling worried—and commenting on Jimmy s responsibility to call her whenever he is going to be late. But there is no guilt tacked on for extra effect. (In a positive, healthy relationship with good communication, there is no need for or benefit from the use of guilt or blame. Responsibility is a more positive tool, and when handled wisely teaches a valuable lesson instead of tearing down self-esteem.)

As a further statement, Mom might say something like this to Jimmy: "Whenever you are going to be late coming home, I want you to be sure to call me. Okay?" Assuming Jimmy then says, "Okay, Mom, I will", they have made a clear complete transaction based on circular communication and I-messages. The matter between them is not only completed satisfactorily, but is done without any leftover guilt or misunderstanding.

The last point I want to make about effective communication is the other side of the coin—*receiving* communication accurately. Obviously, it is not only important to send a clear and appropriate message; it is also important to receive it clearly and know how to respond in a way that indicates you did so.

I think an excellent vehicle for effective listening and responding is the concept of "active listening," now a well-known phrase in the fields of parenting and communication. Some use the terms "reflective" or "attentive" listening to describe very similar ideas. I prefer the term active listening because it indicates not just receiving a message but offering a response that fits, actively involving both the sender and receiver in the response segment of communication.

The truly important point I'd like to make about listening is that it really needs to have full, caring attention. You should be indicating your willingness to be fully present with the other person by being a good listener. The double message of "Yes, I'm listening" when this phrase is spoken as you read the newspaper or watch television is likely to be heard by the other person as "You're not important enough to warrant my full attention." If you, for whatever reason, don't want to or can't give your attention at the time, it's usually best to say so and arrange a time later when you can be fully present with the other person.

Now, regarding the active part of active listening, we're basically talking about letting the other person know you heard them and got the message they intended you to receive. Again, remember that active listening, as with other communication, does not necessarily include agreement with the message—just that your communication process is working.

In active listening, the primary task is to re-state, in your own words—or to feed back—the message you received. This gives the sender the opportunity to know not just that he was heard but that he was heard accurately. For instance, if Johnny comes home from school upset and starts complaining about his teacher, Mrs. Jones, saying "Boy, that Mrs. Jones is the dumbest teacher in the whole world. I can't stand her. I'm never going back to that dumb school; it's awful and so is she," your first reaction might be to defend Mrs. Jones. You may have met her and think she is a nice person and a good teacher. Or perhaps you, as a parent, are afraid that Johnny might try to avoid school from now on and think you should talk him out of it before he gets more serious about the idea.

This is a chance to try active listening instead. You might say to Johnny, "Gee, you're really upset, aren't you? Sounds like you and Mrs. Jones had a rough day at school and you feel mad. I'd like to hear what happened."

In all likelihood, Johnny is going to carry on for a few minutes about the injustices of the day and how he was embarrassed or hurt by something that happened regarding Mrs. Jones. It's also very likely that once he's done that, he will drop the subject and go out to play; and go to school feeling better the next day. What Johnny needs right now is a few minutes of your undivided attention, when he is really listened to and knows it. You not only hear him but let him know that you do, so that he feels your attention and caring. Knowing that you care and that his feelings are acceptable, and having had an opportunity to ventilate his frustrations, Johnny is likely now to be able to let go of his anger and go on with his life.

If he is not heard, he may hang on to his upset feelings until he can do something to complete them in another way. Unexpressed or unaccepted feelings seek a way out of their dilemma of discomfort—they need a sounding board, a caring ear, a sense of legitimacy so they can be let go without leaving remnants of doubt about the experience that created them. If Johnny either keeps his feelings inside or receives disapproval or a lack of attention when he expresses them, he may choose to avoid school, come to hate his teacher or in some other way act out his frustration.

Your willingness to listen to him is validating; it helps Johnny feel okay about his experience and feelings. Even if you think he is distorting what happened, the truth for him is that his experience at school that day was very upsetting and that he needs to deal with his feelings. Your active listening does not imply agreement with his assessment of Mrs. Jones or school. It just lets him know that you understand how it was for him and that his feelings can be handled without him resorting to extremes. Your response will probably result in his eventually taking a wiser look both at what happened and what can be done about it.

You will probably be strongly tempted as a parent to comment on the situation, to "throw in your two cents worth." I see nothing wrong with that, as long as you hear Johnny out first, and you comment in a way that will serve Johnny instead of leaving him feeling badly. Sharing your experiences, even giving an opinion or a suggestion, may be very appropriate and helpful to him. Don't forget to use I-messages, though, and be careful not to preach or lecture.

Remember that your purpose is to let Johnny know that you heard him accurately, as well as to help him look at himself and to better understand his responses to life and its challenges.

Remember that Johnny's problem is his, not yours. Usually we don't help a person by trying to take over, or take on, their problems. We can be more helpful if we leave the responsibility for the problem where it belongs, with the other person, and become a supportive resource instead of a "fixer."

Communication, the vehicle through which we share ourselves and connect and interact with others, is a learned skill. It is extremely important as a tool which, used wisely and well, can make all the difference in the world in the quality and satisfaction of a relationship. Remember, each communication transaction actually is a mini-relationship, in which we are either interacting and relating with another person, or just throwing out a statement and hoping for the best. "Circular" versus "linear" communication shows us the crucial difference between these two methods of communicating.

In the process of sending and receiving, what we are seeking is interacting, not instant compliance or agreement. The use of I-messages and active listening will help foster effective communication as opposed to game-playing or confusion.

Since "you cannot *not* communicate," it is important to do it as well as possible. It may not be easy, especially at first, but with practice, you'll find it becoming second nature in no time. Good luck!

CHAPTER 5
SELF-IMAGE AND SELF-ESTEEM
How To Build Them Up

What do you think is the most important ingredient for good emotional health? There are several possible answers, including a happy and secure family life, feeling loved, having a career that is satsifying, and having friends you feel good about.

But I would say the most essential element which affects emotional development and a person's sense of well-being is high self-esteem.

Before discussing self-esteem, I want to sort out some things that could confuse our understanding of this subject. One of these is the use of two terms which are often used interchangeably but actually mean very different things: self-image and self-esteem.

Self-image is *our identity* as a person. It is the sum of our roles and our perceptions of who we are. For instance, I am a person with various experiences, feelings, and thoughts, a man, Judy's husband, my children's father, Bob's friend, a neighbor of the Smiths', someone who drives a car, a person who plays tennis.

Self-esteem is *our evaluation* of our self-image as being high or low, good or bad, positive or negative, better of worse than that of other people, desirable or unacceptable. It is the assessment you have made about your value in the world, the result of subtle decisions you have made about yourself and impressions you have developed of yourself, such as, "I am well liked" or "I'm not as good as. . ." or "People think of me as being. . . ."

So, if my self-image or identity is that I am a person, a tennis player, a husband, etc., my self-esteem *further* defines me. I begin to see myself as a good person, a poor tennis player, a better husband than the guy next door, an average automobile driver, a well-liked friend, a capable father, someone who is (or is not) *worthwhile and valuable and significant in the world.*

Self-esteem develops over time as you evaluate yourself, consciously or unconsciously. The sum of your feelings, thoughts, experiences and the impressions you receive from others all combine to become what we call self-esteem.

Of course, one's self-esteem develops over time, beginning in earliest infancy and continuing to develop and change all through life. While the adult reaches decisions about self-esteem through role fulfillment, experiences in relationships, use of skills at work or play, and other complex means, for children it is different. An infant or child is likely to base decisions about self-esteem on the amount of positive or nurturing attention he experiences, his sense of whether someone enjoys being with him, how he is held and the results of his early attempts to master tasks. These are subtle but important messages that affect a child's perception of himself in relation to the world.

To summarize, then, self-image is identity; self-esteem is evaluation, a kind of "private rating system" that influences one's emotional development from infancy on and one's sense of well-being all through life.

Let's consider some other points of view about the meaning and importance of self-esteem. Buntman and Saris, in their book, *How To Live With Your Teenager,* say "Self-esteem means a feeling of regard, respect, and affection for oneself." Conversely, we could say that low self-esteem is a low regard or evaluation of oneself.

Dorothy Corkille Briggs, in her excellent book, *Your Child's Self-Esteem,* says "Genuine self-esteem. . .is how you feel about yourself privately, not whether you put up a good front. . . ." Whether a person really feels good about himself cannot be faked to the one who matters most, himself. That is why self-esteem is so important to good emotional health.

How a person feels about himself is a powerful force in determining how that person will live his life. The person with high self-esteem is much more likely to live life with a greater sense of happiness, satisfaction and security than a person with low self-esteem who has doubts about his true value or likeability as a person. In fact, many experts in the fields of psychology and counseling believe that negative behavior can be traced to negative self-esteem, or low self-evaluation. Negative behavior is a statement of how a person sees himself; it is actually a fulfillment or acting out of that person's low self-esteem.

On the other hand, the person with high self-esteem tends to expect and create positive experiences. Positive behavior is a statement of his inner feeling that he deserves good experiences and positive results in life.

The person with a high self-evaluation feels secure about his lovableness and worthwhileness. From this position he can get on with living life happily, with less of a struggle and less doubt than the person with low self-esteem. He has a strong foundation which enables him to be himself, which he sees as good, without the questioning and hesitation an insecure person feels. He feels comfortable pursuing things that increase his self-esteem and which enrich his life.

We have talked about feeling loved and about seeing oneself as lovable. Love is that extremely important but often elusive quality in life which we all seek. Of course, love is one of the bases of healthy self-esteem. The feeling of being loved, and the security that goes with it, is essential to the development of not just a clear self-image but also high self-esteem.

It would be easy to fill many pages with definitions of love, quoting writers and great teachers from Jesus Christ to current leaders in psychology and self-improvement. In a moment I will quote from one historical leader but for now, I'll offer a definition which I believe accurately states the essentials of what love is, especially for our purposes: "Love is caring about a person as they are now, and having a commitment to their well-being." The same definition applies whether one is talking about oneself or others. If you love someone, you are willing to have them be who they are, even if you do not see that as perfect. You care about their welfare and will do all you can to contribute to their well-being, their growth, their health and happiness.

If you truly love yourself, you are willing to accept yourself as you are. You will do all you can to become your best, within your current abilities, but you love yourself now, as you are. If you love your child, you accept him as he is, knowing he is doing the best he is capable of doing, and you are willing to do whatever you can to support him and be with him as he strives to become his best. You have a commitment to this top-quality caring.

As a former minister, I cannot resist the temptation to note here the words of the Apostle Paul, writing in I Corinthians, in the New Testament. He said "Love is patient and kind; love is not jealous and boastful; . . .Love keeps no score of wrongs; . . .There is nothing love cannot face; there is no limit to its faith, its hope and its endurance." I believe he meant that love is not only deeply caring, it is also durable—not fragile or easily endangered. Real love is above pettiness; it does not give in to the small things that can get us off the track. Instead, it is willing to "hang in there" through the events that are not nearly as important as love is.

Your love for someone, whether yourself or someone else, is based on valuing and truly caring for and about that person. It is ideally nonjudgmental and unconditional, for its purpose is not to seek conformity to your wishes with a reward of your love, but rather to let the loved one know he is valued for who he is, whether or not he "deserves" it or has earned it.

You value yourself or another even when you or that person may not be likeable at the moment. Hopefully, your loved one knows that he or she has inherent worth to you. Your willingness to love, and your actions in loving, are choices you've made and something you want to do. The question you must answer is how to do it the best you can, with other adults and with your children.

A relationship built on this kind of caring love will be mutually supportive because the people truly care about and want the best for each other. Each person wants to feel that he, as well as the people with whom he is involved, is inherently lovable and worthwhile. This is not conditioned on anything except being. In other words, you love someone even when you differ, when one person makes a mistake or when you don't like an action committed by the other. You do not need to worry about every single thing in your life together because what the other person believes or feels does not determine whether he is of value to you. True love is not cancelled by external events, disagreements or differences of opinion about such minor things as hair length, clothes style or musical preferences. These things are not the essence of a person; they are just things that tell us people are different.

Love, then, is support, commitment to one another, mutual caring, the desire for well-being, and the intention to have a relationship because you want to. It is not power, possession or attachment; the things that make people compete and feel conditional, fearing they will "lose" if they are not careful.

What is the opposite of love? It is not hate, as is so often thought. Hate may be a fleeting experience because we care enough to feel strongly for a moment. Hate can also be a sign of great emotional upheaval or even emotional illness in extreme cases. But it is not the true opposite of love; that is apathy or in-difference.

I know it is sometimes very hard to love someone who is not being very lovable or perhaps not even likeable. It is ironic that these are often the times when people, especially children, most need to be loved!

While loving and liking are related, they are not the same and don't necessarily even go together. For instance, in friendships we don't always love those we like, but we still care about them. In family relationships we don't always like those we love, but we still love them. In fact, we may at times feel we don't even love those we love! I think that's alright, assuming it's just a passing feeling—after all, we do have human limitations despite our best intentions.

So how do we help our children develop positive self-esteem? The essential task is to help them experience themselves as lovable and worthwhile; to help them develop a belief that they are inherently valuable. We need to help them distinguish between being loved because they did something "right" and being loved because they are yours and you love them for who they are.

Encourage your children both to be themselves and to live up to their potential, but be careful not to overly pressure them. You could set up a power struggle that won't serve you or them well. Acknowledge them for their assets more often than you criticize them for their liabilities. Let them know you appreciate their uniqueness and recognize their accomplishments. But don't lavish them with so much praise that they feel they must always be doing something "good" or they won't get any attention or recognition.

Interestingly, praise can be a manipulative tool, even a negative element in a relationship, if it is not handled well. Instead of being used to build self-esteem, it could be a parent's way of manipulating a child to do what the parent wants him to do. The child may eventually get the idea that if he doesn't do what Mom or Dad wants, he won't be praised, which he needs to feel good about himself. The object of the child's behavior would then be to receive praise, sometimes at the expense of being himself. He needs to find ways to be acknowledged for his own personality and for the things he can do that are praise-worthy.*

---

*Dinkmeyer and McKay, in *The Parent's Handbook—S.T.E.P.*, effectively speak about these points and suggest specific

As another way to enhance your child's self-esteem, be willing to believe the best about your child and his ability to do well; have a positive attitude and positive expectations. Don't worry that the result of your positive beliefs are not always what you hope for—that's not the point. Your expectations are powerful forces which can greatly influence a child. If they are positive, those expectations can be very supportive, as long as they are not conditional. The child shouldn't feel he is a failure if he doesn't satisfy your "picture" of how he should be.

Positive attitude = positive outcome. This is not a formula with a guarantee of perfection, but you are going to get more positive outcomes with it than you are likely to get without it. Belief in a person's ability actually helps bring about positive growth in that person. For instance, your trust contributes toward building trustworthiness in your child. Your belief that your child is good and worthwhile helps him build the foundation that will support the best possible outcome in his life.

What I am talking about is offering children a *climate* in which to develop the best side of themselves. This means helping them to be aware of possibilities and doing what you can to give them opportunities for satisfaction through successful experiences. It means showing them that the most important person in their world—their parent—knows, loves and believes in them and feels they deserve to succeed and be happy.

Briggs suggests parents realize their importance as image-builders by envisioning themselves as "mirrors" in which their children "see" themselves. The reflections they get from you influence their view of themselves. For example, if you mirror to them that you think they are lovable, then they see themselves as being lovable. On the other hand, if they perceive from you that they are troublesome, then that will also affect how they see themselves. If you are warm and responsive, they get a very different "picture" of who they are and how valuable they are than they do if you are cool, distant, and often preoccupied. How you behave toward your children is how they will tend to see themselves, and this becomes a significant source of data which they use to develop their self-image and self-esteem.

It is not just these specific messages that are important, but also the overall tone of the environment in which children live that is significant. A generally nurturing environment conveys love and security, and promotes a sense of well-being, even when

---

ways you can give encouragement to your child.

there are occasional moments of tension or disagreement. A cool or unfeeling environment which seems to tell a child, "It's risky to get close", or "I'm too busy (for you). . ." conveys another kind of message; one which isn't likely to be overshadowed even when there are occasional moments of love and security.

In a similar vein, the amount of attention and its quality tell a child a lot about how you feel about his value, not just to you but to other people. Whether we like it or not, we do represent to our children much more than ourselves—we represent what they can expect for themselves the rest of their lives.

Giving your child attention just for being who he is, just because you care about him—nobody said anything about him being perfect—is ideal. It says, "You matter to me." The assumption the child is likely to make is, then, "I matter to people; I'm worthwhile in this world."

When you respect your child, and his feelings and opinions, you say to him, "You are important", and convey to him that "You don't have to agree or feel exactly the way I do for your feelings and opinions to be as worthwhile as anyone else's." A child whose feelings, thoughts and experiences are given importance learns to trust them, evaluate them, and then validate them on his own as he grows. He learns that his experiences are important just because they are his, whether or not the people around him agree with him. Disagreements between people can be handled much better when each person respects the validity of the other's experiences. Each person is then free to seek a solution to life's problems without having to defend his position.

In my workshop for parents on handling stress and avoiding burnout, I suggest that people develop their own "personal affirmations." (For a more detailed treatment of this subject, see Chapter 3 of this book.) My definition of personal affirmations is that they are statements which are true about you and the intentions you have for your life. Some adult affirmations might be: "I will love myself as much as I can", or "It is important for me to be in the best possible physical condition", or "I intend to spend more time with my family in the next six months." These are statements which affirm something you already are aware of or are working to incorporate into your life, or things you intend to work on in the future.

Consider developing some affirmations for yourself as an individual and as a parent. Also consider developing statements for, or with, your children—things that will help them feel confirmed as people who are lovable and worthwhile. These could be statements you keep in your mind about how you view, or would like to view, your children. They can be goals about how you would like to interact with them as they grow, or concepts you believe would be useful for them in affirming themselves.

Helping your children develop and incorporate affirmations for themselves could be a good learning experience and a useful lifelong practice. Jean Illsley Clark, in her book, *Self-Esteem, A Family Affair*, discusses affirmations, "strokes" and visualizations for positive growth and relates these to each age and developmental group (see, for instance, pages 34-37 in her book). She also offers ideas on how to avoid negative messages, or "Don't Be" messages, as she calls them, and how to give messages that confirm a child is acceptable.

Good self-image and self-esteem, productive communication and effective discipline—the three areas covered in this section—comprise the three most important areas a parent needs to understand and practice effectively.

As a final note about self-esteem, it might be interesting and useful to you as a parent to take inventory of the status of your own self-esteem. Perhaps you will gain some insights that will help you deal more effectively with your children. Or, you may find that areas of your own self-esteem need attention in order for you to experience more of the sense of happiness and satisfaction that we all need to feel our best and perform at our highest level.

CHAPTER 6
RULES AND DISCIPLINE
Authoritative vs Authoritarian

Several years ago I read of an incident that still amuses me when I recall it. Great Britain's Duke of Windsor, Edward, was visiting our country, observing life and the people of America. Near the end of his visit he was asked by a reporter for some observations and comments on his time here. Among Edward's comments was, "The thing that impresses me most about America is the way parents obey their children!"

For many people that comment may seem too close to home to be funny. But it does illustrate a point that parents may identify with more than they would like—at times it seems that children *are* running the show more than parents would like. Some parents, not knowing what to do about this, eventually give in to feelings of resignation. "What's the use?" they think to themselves when they are overwhelmed with the struggles of parenting. Perhaps their early feelings of happiness and satisfaction as parents give way to resentment and frustration as they wonder if they have somehow failed.

For most people there is no aspect of parenting as likely to evoke this feeling as the area of rules and discipline. Parents' concern about the need to teach effective discipline to their children is heightened by the complexity of the world today and the seriousness of its temptations.

Every generation has complained that things are worse, different, more confusing. Usually this viewpoint is accompanied by nostalgia for "the good old days." These feelings are another way of expressing concern about constant change, which is often hard to cope with.

But those of us living in the 1980s really *do* face unique challenges as parents. The world really *has* changed; it is different than when we grew up, different than we thought it would be for raising our children. The concept of authority doesn't have the same meaning or carry the same weight it did when we were children. Saying "do it just because I said to" doesn't get the results we expect, and we—wisely—have second thoughts about hitting or spanking children as a regular means of discipline. (I believe that hitting or spanking is virtually never a wise choice. It teaches that physical means are okay to enforce one's views or demands, or to express frustration. Too often it has resulted in physical harm or abuse which the parent did not originally intend to happen.)

What is discipline? While dictionaries vary somewhat in defining the word, most say discipline involves things like: training; a system of control; lessons in self-control; rules for conduct; a system for correction or punishment; and a means to enforce standards.

I would say the clearest, simplest definition of discipline and its purpose, especially as applied to parenting, would be to say that it is training for self-discipline. In other words, the primary reason for parents to use disciplinary practices is to help their children grow into self-disciplined, self-guided individuals. Ideally, it is the parent's goal to work him or herself out of the job of disciplinarian.

How do you effectively train children to be self-disciplined? You should set an example and use disciplinary practices that include the essentials you would like your child to understand and use, including things like good communication, healthy self-image and self-esteem, a sense of fairness and responsibility coupled with respect for self and others, and an understanding of the need for basic rules in society (and the consequences of breaking rules).

You might not realize it, but as an individual you bring a lot to your parenting role, such as your personal history, experiences and beliefs, which exert strong and varied influences. How you were raised and treated as a child, how you now view the world, and your beliefs about why people behave as they do will affect your parenting role.

Of particular importance is how power and authority have been experienced in your life. While we have the ability and the right to question and change many things, it is often true that how our parents used power and authority will influence how we use power with our own children in their early years. It will also affect how our children deal with these issues in their adolescent years and later.

The more authoritarian a parent has been toward a child, especially if the parent is seen as very rigid and unresponsive, the more likely the parent is to have difficulty, especially during his child's adolescence. Many teenagers delight in challenging rigid authority to see where the breaking point is, to discover how much they can get away with. (Adults do it too—that's why we have laws for everything from running red traffic lights to income tax fraud.)

On the other hand, if a parent is very permissive, imposing few limits, expectations or structure upon the child, that also can present problems because children need appropriate guidelines within which to operate. A child can feel lost and anxious without the right guidance suited to his age and situation.

The ideal falls somewhere between the two extremes. I believe that a parent needs to consider very carefully what his position is regarding rules, discipline, power and authority; only then can policies be established and practiced effectively. As a way to begin looking at these areas, I suggest that parents ask themselves three questions:

- In what ways am I willing or not willing to allow input from others, especially my children, regarding rules and discipline; how do I feel about a democratic approach as compared to a more authoritarian one?

- What do I know about myself regarding rules, discipline, power, authority, my views about flexibility, firmness, consistency and rigidity that may influence the course of rules and disciplinary issues for my family?

- What rules, limits and basic policies do I think are important, and ones which I must insist on, regardless of the kind of approach my family takes toward discipline?

After answering these questions as honestly as possible, you will be more ready to examine the best way to approach a workable policy and method of discipline for your family. This should be based not just on what you think is best or what you "should" do, but also on what you know about yourself.

I believe a general policy which makes sense is what I call "authoritative democracy." While parents will apply this idea in different ways, depending on their personal preferences and family situation, the underlying principle is to share some of both the power and the responsibilities of discipline in parenting in ways appropriate to the ages and abilities of the children.

Certainly this does *not* mean all parental responsibility or authority is given over to the children in a family. Responsible parents will still need to exercise wise controls and demands when appropriate. The question is this: Will you be more authoritative than authoritarian, or vice versa? Let's look more closely at the differences between these words, which look similar but have very different meanings.

To be *authoritative* is to have authority—legitimate or competent authority, the dictionary calls it—but to choose to share it in certain ways.

To be *authoritarian* is to believe in, or attempt to enforce absolute authority.

Which of these approaches seems most likely to you to help a child learn to practice healthy self-discipline and develop responsibility and self-respect? I believe the authoritative approach offers both the attitude and the methods most likely to produce the best results.

When a person is invited to share power, with a sense of equality and responsibility, this encourages that person's growth and self-respect. But when he is expected only to follow the rules laid down by others, either rebellion against, or dependency on, those rules and the people enforcing them is likely to occur. In raising children we are seeking not to develop rebellion or dependency, but to teach healthy self-discipline. There should be a sense of responsibility and participation in a system that works well for all concerned. I believe that authoritative democracy is an important part of this.

When we talk of authoritative democracy, a system based on involving everyone in some way in the issues of rules and discipline, we are not talking about having no rules or limits in a family. Rather, we are talking about how rules are established most effectively, how breaking of those rules is handled, and deciding what the children's roles should be in the process.

In a family in which children have at least some voice in

setting rules and determining the consequences when the rules are broken, those children tend to become more responsible. They have a genuine stake in the whole situation, which puts them in a very different position from children who are simply given orders and expected to follow them without question.

It stands to reason, then, that children in a family which is run more like an authoritative democracy than an authoritarian regime are not as likely to need to test limits or break rules because they helped set them in the first place, and can have some say in changing them if necessary. These children feel less need to rebel against or try to outsmart the system because they are part of it. Thus they are not likely to feel the powerlessness or resentment against authority that often leads to rebellion.

It is difficult for many parents to consider the notion of giving up some of their power. They may feel that if they are not in charge, then their children will be. Others feel it is the duty, right and responsibility of parents to be in control; they argue that their children need this from them since, as parents, they have greater knowledge and experience.

How much you are willing to share, and how you and your children go about setting up a system that will serve you best as a family is largely up to you, since personalities, needs and problems vary so much from family to family. However, some suggestions follow, and for more ideas you can refer to some of the books in the suggested reading list at the end of this book.

I think families used to do more together than they do today. They shared more meals, went on more outings, trips and picnics, played games and visited relatives together more than we do today. In past years (especially before television's strong influence), more casual visiting went on and issues were discussed more frequently. Problems were solved in the course of just spending time together. The complex and busy times in which we live now seem almost to require that appointments be made to see members of one's own family. Many people feel they don't have much time to be with each other or talk over things, so too many issues go undiscussed, causing great frustration.

Families need a time just to be together, to chat casually or socialize, to air gripes and to discuss and attempt to solve problems. They need time to plan vacations or holiday events, assign or change chores, set family rules, discuss allowances or talk about a disliked babysitter.

A growing number of people are doing this by having family meetings. These meetings bear a lot of resemblance to the less structured time families used to spend together, back in the "good old days," before life seemed to get so complicated.

Not only are family meetings good for just spending time together, but they are also a good place to discuss problems and reach agreements. During these meetings families can actually practice a system involving authoritative democracy.

An ideal length for a family meeting is thirty to sixty minutes, and a suggested frequency is once a week—more if possible or necessary during a crisis—preferably the same day and time each week so people can plan around it. Someone should keep minutes, perhaps a different family member each time. Meetings should be orderly but comfortably informal, with enough structure to serve the purpose of handling issues. Everyone should be encouraged to comment, express concerns and offer problems for discussion.

I would suggest several steps which might make your family meetings more effective:

- Identify current concerns that should be on the agenda. Make a list of these, knowing that some weeks this list of topics will be short, other weeks long. In either case, this first step will give an indication right away of the current "condition" and mood of the family.

- Clarify, as needed, any doubts about the meaning of any item on the list, asking for more information if necessary, to avoid misunderstandings or incorrect assumptions.

- Choose what items will be discussed at this meeting if it appears everything cannot be covered. If some items won't be covered at this meeting, give them priority at the next one.

- Brainstorm each topic for possible solutions, discussing as much as is necessary to get at all relevant points and possible solutions. Draw out quieter family members who may have trouble speaking out but seem to have something to say. The minutes-keeper should note the major points and suggestions made.

- Narrow down and negotiate the possible solutions that emerge as most worthy of final consideration. By now, the family should be getting close to a final solution everyone can live with. The art of compromise, involving discussion, negotiation, and give-and-take, all done in good faith, is part of this step. Look for areas in which people are in agreement or have similar views. See what they can live with or give up comfortably and what seems most or least important as indicators of the direction negotiations can take for a final, successful conclusion to each item.

- Reach agreements and note what they are accurately in the minutes. Be clear as to who will do what, how, when and any other pertinent details to avoid misunderstandings later.

- Review the meeting briefly just before it ends. But resist the temptation to use this time for reworking items or trying to convince someone who seems to be wavering on a point. If someone is having reservations, perhaps a workable agreement has not really been reached on that item. If reopening discussion on a topic is necessary, arrange to do it at the next meeting when there is time and minds are fresh.

Routine points, such as a minor change in chore duties, may take only a few minutes before an acceptable agreement is reached. A lengthy discussion on some point may take several weeks. For these more complex discussions it is often a good idea to make a contract-like written agreement after a solution is found. This not only preserves the details of each item accurately; it lends a feeling of formality that encourages compliance and adult responsibility.

If a written contractual agreement is going to be used, I suggest you go all the way to get the most benefit from it. It should be divided into sections as appropriate, properly worded, typed, and signed by all parties. Then, everyone should receive a copy of it.

One family I worked with had a difficult time talking things over calmly and in an orderly way, especially when the subject touched any problem area—of which there were many, in their opinion. When they talked, whether in my office or at home, they had a hard time staying on a subject, had a tendency to be accusatory and argumentative even when they didn't intend to be, and talked too long on most subjects, thus losing the attention of the other family members.

These people—Mom, Dad, teenage son, John, and the daughter, who was away at college—are all bright, outspoken and high-energy individuals who care a lot about each other. They just couldn't seem to identify, discuss, or reach agreement on a number of concerns which they knew needed attention. Most of these areas concerned John, but some were about the whole family's interactions and their ways of treating each other.

It became clear as time went on that some means of resolving their complex situation was needed. When I explained, then suggested, the idea of a written contractual agreement, they immediately thought it was a good idea. The four weeks it took to work it all out in my office were at times rocky, to say the least, but I knew it could be very useful if everyone would just stick with the job. They did and it was.

What follows is their agreement, item by item, which was recorded, typed, copied, and signed. The agreement is used here with this family's permission, but I have changed names and minor details to protect their identities.

AGREEMENT

THE UNDERSIGNED PARTIES AGREE AS FOLLOWS:

I. **HOMEWORK AND SCHOOL**
   A. John will keep a weekly graph of school assignments.
   B. Parents can see the graph on Tuesdays, Thursdays, and once on weekends if they wish (so they will know John's current status regarding upcoming school assignments).
   C. It is agreed schoolwork matters are essentially John's responsibility; parents and others are to be resource people for him and his responsibilities.

D. A grade of B- or better earns increased privileges. A grade of D or worse means fewer privileges as a general rule.

II. CONDITION OF ROOM, ETC.
A. John will do his own laundry, per his own wishes, each Saturday or Sunday.
B. John will put his dirty clothes in the hamper once each day (or more frequently if he chooses, but more frequently is not required by parents).
C. John will keep his room clean, up to agreed-upon standards understood by all.

III. MONEY — DISTRIBUTION AND USE
A. John will be paid $7 per week for doing dishes every other day and bringing in the garbage can once each week, and an additional $5 per hour for any additional jobs completed over and above these two jobs.
B. Parents will not require an accounting of how John's money is spent AND will not be asked for additional money if John overspends at times.

IV. TREATMENT OF PARENTS AND OTHER FAMILY MEMBERS
A. John agrees to handle his responsibilities consistently and well. His parents will not check up on him unless an extreme situation comes to their attention which in their judgment requires their intervention for his or others' safety.
B. John and Father will both make extra efforts to be polite to Mother, especially when not in a "good mood," and will cease all "name calling" or derogatory statements regarding any family member.
C. Mother will recognize John's and Father's needs for individual space and time to themselves; all will attempt to express what they need at appropriate times (communicate effectively rather than act out feelings of dissatisfaction).
D. All agree to make efforts to respect each other's uniqueness and try not to side with any family member against another.

V. CHURCH ATTENDANCE

A. John will decide and tell parents no later than Saturday evening whether he will go with them to church the next day. It is understood he will usually attend but can decline with advance notice.

VI. TREATMENT OF SISTER

A. John agrees to practice self-restraint in his relationship with his sister, particularly in situations where he is aware an argument is beginning. He will make every effort not to antagonize her, initiate or start arguments and will make every effort to stop any that may begin. He will ask his sister not to talk to him in the mornings, when he feels especially "grumpy."

VII. SKI CLUB

A. John will come home directly (without delay) from school on Friday afternoons when he has a ski club trip the next day, in order to rest. If he goes out these evenings, he will be home no later than 9:00 p.m. or forfeit his ski trip the next day.

VIII. TELEVISION USE AND FREQUENCY

A. There will be no television watching Sunday through Thursday evenings.

B. On Friday and Saturday, John can watch three hours of daytime television and can have unlimited viewing from 6:00 p.m. on (except on ski club Friday evenings).

IX. FRIENDS

A. Mother notes and John acknowledges she has some remaining concerns regarding John's choice of friends and their influence on him. This is noted here "for the record."

All parties, including me as mediator and family therapist, signed and received a copy of this agreement.

Most family meetings will not need to cover such a wide range of topics regarding one member, or put together an agreement as extensive as this one. However, the details presented here illustrate the extent of detail you may need to cover in order to deal with a topic adequately. This particular agreement actually covers not just agreements about John but some about his parents and the family's interactions. It is to everyone's credit that they were willing to recognize the need for this and that they addressed these issues in a way that worked for all concerned.

One of the keys to making this system work is to have good communication (discussed in detail in Chapter 4). Closely related to this is the need to be on the alert for, and be prepared to deal with, not just what is said but with the feelings involved in a situation. It is likely that at times family meetings, like daily life, will present situations where there are conflicting or confusing feelings which need to be sorted out and dealt with, or at least acknowledged. In fact, the feelings involved in a situation are often a better indication of what is really going on than is the actual problem being discussed. It is at these times that parents may need to assume a greater role, offering extra help and support, to help identify and cope with these underlying feelings.

Finally, as mentioned earlier, effective coping with a potentially sticky issue necessitates being clear about who "owns" a problem or has responsibility for handling a certain matter. If the problem belongs to your child, don't get needlessly involved in it, except as a resource person. If it is yours, or involves you, then proceed accordingly.

There may be times when a method which I call the "matter-of-fact approach" may be called for. When a crisis exists, emotions are running high, or people are tired or just not coping well, this approach may be best. It is at these times that it is important to avoid getting entangled by events or statements. Typically, we get distracted or upset when we are feeling let down, when an agreement has been broken or when someone is behaving in a way that scares or shocks us. It is easy at these times to react, when we really should respond wisely instead. A reaction is more of an automatic act, whereas a response is a considered choice, consciously made.

Taking a matter-of-fact attitude and approach allows you to shift gears to a method of coping that may allow for a different outcome to the situation. This is not to suggest that you should be uncaring or uninvolved; only that you should stand back a little and regain perspective. This helps you take charge of yourself during difficult times, to avoid getting caught up in the emotion of the moment, which might cloud your good judgment.

Another benefit of this approach is that because you stay calmer, you don't pay too much attention to negative behavior. When you focus on someone's negative behavior, this can actually reinforce or draw attention to it. Being clear-headed also allows you to stay out of certain problems that your child needs to resolve by himself. As hard as it is to admit sometimes, all things that occur in our children's lives—especially those we really can't do anything about—are not necessarily our problem or responsibility to handle. Getting involved in them may not only make them worse but could unnecessarily strain your relationship with your child.

It is important for parents to understand their own limitations and to be aware of their priorities and long-term goals. This can be helpful in staying calm about a particular situation and perhaps realizing that one event is not likely to have an earth-shaking impact on our children's lives.

Then again, parents should be alert to problems that require an authoritative intervention. It's alright to be a confident, secure parent and to intervene with effective parental authority when that is the sensible and necessary thing to do. Clear, effective demands are sometimes the only appropriate action to take and we owe it to ourselves and our children to know when and how to use these demands well.*

Don't be afraid of your children or your task as a parent, or seek to have them fear you; insecurity and resentment are likely to occur. Do give your children your full respect and expect respect from them. Remember that your example is a powerful teaching tool.

How are children turn out is, in a very real sense, a shared responsibility between us and them. There are no guarantees, but the more we give them a sound, positive base, encouraging and guiding them the best we can, the better they can build on that result, creating sound, happy lives.

Finally, remember that the goal of parental discipline is to teach wise self-discipline.

---

*How To Get Your Children To Do What You Want Them To do, by Wood and Schwartz, provides an interesting treatment of this subject. Bodenhamer's Back In Control is another good book. He states that there are three basic parts to getting children to do what's required of them: parents need to clearly state their rules, demands or requests; effectively follow through; and be consistent. The author applies these basics to a number of situations parents face, especially parents of older children and teens, including those with serious behavior problems.

SECTION III
DESERVING OF SPECIAL ATTENTION

CHAPTER 7
SINGLE PARENTS
The Toughest Job

The Carters are, in many ways, typical of many American families today. They moved to the fast-growing, yet still quiet and safe suburban community just forty miles from San Francisco to get away from the hustle and bustle of a big city. It was close enough for Dad to commute to work and seemed a good place to raise kids—good schools, beautiful neighborhoods, many shopping centers. Admittedly, it was rather expensive and would require some sacrifices to live there.

Mr. Carter had a good job as a junior executive for a major retail store and some solid opportunities for advancement. Mrs. Carter worked awhile but found it impossible to keep up with the tasks at home, with four children, a house to maintain, two cars and three pets. She and her husband eventually decided that it was best that she quit her job and stay home. But they soon realized that he would have to moonlight at a second job whenever he could to make ends meet.

After a couple of years of this schedule, the strain began to show. As the children, two of them adopted as infants, grew older, the complications of family life grew. Mrs. Carter was overwhelmed much of the time and starved for adult company. Mr. Carter was always tired when he was home. The children developed their own lives, often apart from family activities which became more difficult to arrange. Mr. and Mrs. Carter became more aware that their life together lacked satisfaction and that the little time they did have was spent talking about kids and problems, money and things to be fixed around the house. By the time they realized how serious their problems were, how much their marriage was strained as a result of their chosen lifestyle, it was too late. Instead of seeking help, they drifted further apart and decided to separate. A year later they decided to divorce, feeling that counseling would probably not help and that they preferred to live without each other anyway.

About two years after the divorce, they wished they had tried to save the marriage, but it was not a workable option, so they continued to do their best to make their separate lives work. It wasn't easy. Mrs. Carter had all four children living with her and she worked at a full-time job. She liked the job quite well but it took a lot out of her to work all day, then come home and cook and take care of the children, handle the housework, pets and all the rest. Mr. Carter was basically a responsible father who usually paid child support on time, visited the children regularly and did his best to let them know he cared about them.

The Carters' situation is not an ideal one by any means, but it is much better than many others. At least they were able to provide their children with the basic necessities of life and an occasional treat or outing, and they both did their best to meet their parental responsibilities. They tried to be considerate of each other despite some of the leftover feelings of guilt, doubt, and resentment that often occur with divorce.

The increasing incidence of divorce may be the fastest growing trend in American life in the last twenty years. From being relatively rare it has become quite common, especially in large urban or suburban areas, like the Carters' seemingly ideal suburban, tree-lined community.

As you probably know, about one in two marriages ends in divorce today, especially in California and other states' metropolitan areas. Perhaps the only consolation in this otherwise bleak fact is that at least divorce does not carry quite the stigma it once did, since it seems everybody's doing it. But that doesn't mean it is any less painful or scary today.

One of the results of the growing divorce rate is that there are now a great many single-parent households—almost four million at last count. And almost ninety percent of the heads of these households are women (although there is an increasing—and I think healthy—trend toward father-led single-parent households).

If being a parent is one of the hardest, most responsible jobs in the world, being a good single parent is even more so. If a single parent works, has limited finances, or other related stresses, which most do, then the job of parenting can seem overwhelming.

There are certainly single parents, as with any other category of parents, who do not find the tasks they face overly difficut. Some even prefer their situation and do the job well, without any apparent problems for them or their children. These may be the people who prefer not to have to share their time or "space" with another adult unless they choose to, or who prefer the single life to what they see as the hassles of marriage. They may have unlimited energy or love to have time alone with their children or friends.

But these single parents are probably in the minority. Most find it a difficult task. The problems that most single parents face often include the following:

- In a very real sense a single parent is, on a day-to-day basis, both mother and father to the children, even if the absent parent is fairly involved with and supportive of the children and the former partner.

- The single parent is often doing alone the job *two* people can find overwhelming at times.

- He or she is doing this job without the daily support and help that a mate usually offers.

- A single parent is living singly in a world that is basically still structured for couples and often is very aware of this "different" status.

- There are often financial hardships, feelings of being stuck in a less-than-exciting job, or other things that leave the single parent feeling unsatisfied.

- Finally, both parties to a divorce often feel guilt, loneliness, or a sense of hopelessness, which is bound to hinder their effectiveness in building a new life and doing their best job as a parent.

Of course, not all single parents are single because of divorce. Some are single because of the death of a spouse, are married but the spouse is working or on military duty out of the country, or are single by choice.

Some people begin their life as a single parent reeling at the difficulties they face, but find they can rise to the occasion very well and can be successful. In fact, this is a more possible outcome than most people realize. But it is not likely to come easily, or without some soul-searching and careful, focused effort.

When I'm counseling a single parent, especially one who is faced with any of the added stresses I mentioned earlier, I encourage him or her to be aware of these things and to acknowledge the potential difficulty of the task he or she faces. This is not to make the single parent feel worse, only to help him be realistic, to resist the temptation to deny potential problem areas, and to plan his life wisely.

As a single parent it is important for you to learn to take good care of not only your children but also to take the best possible care of yourself. Your needs should be met and you should build into your life opportunities for rest and recuperation. This does not occur automatically, will probably not be easy, and may require creative measures and dogged determination to accomplish it.

Certainly the single parent is not the only candidate for parental burnout; parents of teens, stepparents, and those with demanding careers are all close seconds. But single parents have a unique need to be careful to prevent burnout because of their singleness; because they lack a mate to share the burdens that can contribute to stress and burnout.

Since the single parent is essentially mateless, even if there is a former spouse nearby who shares some of the parenting role, it is important for most to do something to make up for this lack of a resident co-parent. One way to do this is to enlist the help and support of the former spouse if at all possible. Some divorced parents have joint-custody arrangements, in which each has the children about half of the time. This is fine if their relationship allows it, they live near each other, and their jobs and other responsibilities dovetail in ways that make it possible. But most couples don't seem able to work out such an arrangement, or make it work well over a long period of time. Some experts even feel this is not the best situation for the children since it may make them feel they don't have a home—one place where they can feel their life is centered, where all their personal belongings and friends are. There is a growing trend toward various kinds of joint custody arrangements and it may prove a workable alternative for families in the future.

Another way single parents can compensate for the lack of a partner is to develop support systems involving extended family or other single parents. I often encourage parents—whether married or single—to develop the best possible relationship with other relatives, especially grandparents or favorite aunts and uncles—people children usually benefit from being close to in any circumstance. While these relationships are not always ideal, and may have their own stresses, it is often possible to iron out rough spots so these family members can be more available and more helpful to both parent and children.

Even if extended family members live in another state, consider the possibility of visiting them during the summer. This can be a respite for you and an opportunity for your children to develop their relationships with these family members. Or perhaps grandparents or an aunt and uncle could visit your home or stay nearby. Let them help out with housework, cooking, or errands, or trips to an amusement park with the children if they are at all willing to do so.

One family I worked with had no family members near them since the family—Mom, Dad and one child—moved to California from Florida to take advantage of a job opportunity soon after their child was born. Now, divorced and living many miles from any family, the mother saves a little out of her paycheck each month to finance alternate-year visits to Florida where she visits for a week, then leaves her son who, at age twelve, enjoys flying home by himself a month later. When she doesn't go to Florida, her retired parents come to California and stay for about a month. Fortunately, they love to help around the house, so they take over many of the household chores while visiting. And, of course, they enjoy spoiling their grandson. The occasional strain between this mother and her parents, and the need she feels to "un-spoil" her son for about a week after their visits, are a small price to pay for the benefits which result from these annual summer get-togethers.

Some families allow their children to go on vacations with other family members, perhaps to travel with grandparents or go camping with other relatives. Don't forget the possibility of your children visiting an ex-spouse's family. It is important for children to maintain ties with your ex-spouse's parents, if at all possible.

Summer camp is another means to gain respite and a change in routine for you and your children. A Scout campout, church group outing, community recreation department day-camp, or even summer school can also be worthwhile.

Something many parents could consider is developing a network of other single parents with whom they trade off parenting time. This can be done in a variety of ways. For instance, you might take another parent's children for a weekend and they would take yours another time. Or, you and another parent could take all the children on a camping trip. You might want to start a single parents' support group where you meet regularly for discussion, mutual support, invite outside speakers and have occasional group outings. At meetings, the participating parents could discuss problem-solving—what has worked or not worked for someone else can be a valuable resource of information—suggest books or magazine articles that have been helpful, share ideas about hobbies or outside interests that are satisfying, or develop a network of child-sharing. A support group can also serve just as an opportunity for socializing, for both parents and the children.

In summary, don't be afraid to seek out what you need. Try different things, ask for help, share your problems and feelings when you can, especially during times of stress. Don't wait for stressful times; build your resources and support systems now so they will be there when you need them. Having resources available could mean that stress will occur less often.

Mrs. Carter, whom I spoke of at the beginning of this chapter, once waited too long to take care of herself. I'd like to share her story with you as an example of "creative coping" which had a happy ending.

Almost two years after she and her husband divorced, Mrs. Carter (I'll call her Joyce) was feeling particularly exhausted and was having some serious problems coping with her single parent role. Two of her children were having difficulty in school and one had been caught shoplifting recently. They missed their father, fought with each other a lot, and generally showed some of the signs of strain which Joyce also felt. At one point she wondered if she could, or even was willing to, go on with her single parenting any longer. Because of tight finances, it was not possible to do what she really wanted to do—and knew would help very much—which was to take a vacation for a week or two. She wanted to be by herself, to catch up on reading, loafing, and just thinking.

It was clear to me that she had to take action, or something would snap in her family's life together. As we talked about this for a couple of weeks, it was obvious she really needed a vacation but that there was no way to have it—the money just wasn't there. So I asked her how much she could come up with in a week to ten days if she had to. She said she could "borrow" about thirty-five, or at the most forty, dollars from the household money, if necessary. I encouraged her to arrange that and to let me know the following week when she could have the money.

At our next meeting, Joyce said she had arranged to have the funds available any time. We then discussed what she could do for herself with a maximum of forty dollars. We decided that what she most wanted was to get away by herself. Fortunately, she had a friend who lived nearby who was willing to take Joyce's children for a weekend. So, we decided together that she would go to a small town about fifty miles away. In a telephone directory, we found a motel that was part of a nationwide chain of budget motels that were very basic, but clean, and usually located next to inexpensive coffee shops. The following weekend Joyce left her children with the friend and went to the motel for two nights, taking reading material, walking shoes, a large amount of picnic supplies and enough money to eat in the coffee shop for two meals.

Joyce came back from her weekend retreat a different person. She had slept ten hours a night, caught up on her reading and went for two walks a day by herself. She felt she had had a royal treat because she ate two meals out—something she seldom does. It was perhaps the best forty dollars she had ever spent.

It may not be easy, but it is usually possible for everyone to find some way to take better care of themselves. For both single and other parents, this could be a very important step toward becoming both a happier person and a better parent.

CHAPTER 8
STEPPARENTING
A Little Different Challenge

Being a stepparent is both the same as *and* a lot different than "regular" parenting. I think most stepparents would agree with this statement after just a short time in their new role.

With the rise in divorce has come not just an increase in single-parent families but also another type of family—the blended family. Blended families are becoming a major force in American society today; a fact which is evident if you consider just the sheer numbers. The latest estimates indicate that almost forty million people live in blended families—about fifteen million children and twenty-five million adults or stepparents. Given a U.S. population of about 230 million people, that means about one in six people in our country lives in a blended family as a stepchild or stepparent.

I think one reason this phenomenon is growing, besides the obvious fact that divorce is so common, is that people are pairing or marrying creatures. They seek a family experience, sharing and intimacy, even if they've had a painful experience with it before. People tend to want to have the closeness, security and satisfaction that marriage and family life can offer.

Some people, being insecure or afraid of failure, choose to live together without marriage, at least for a while. Interestingly, these people often find themselves plagued by the same dynamics and problems faced by married couples. This chapter is offered to all couples living in stepfamily arrangements, married or not, because the situations they face are so similar.

I write this not just as a professional—as a clinical social worker and family therapist for many years—but as one with personal experience. I have been through divorce and experienced the pain and confusion that go with it. I know about the deep, wrenching feeling of missing my children and some of the experiences we could have had "growing up together" in the same household. Fortunately, my former wife and I have had a good co-parenting relationship and she and my children's stepfather have been a very good parenting team as well. During these years since the divorce, my children and I have remained very close and involved with each other, have lived near each other, and have had frequent contacts.

I have experienced being a "single parent" as a weekend and vacation parent. Since remarrying, I've experienced the step-parent role also, in two ways — my children have spent a lot of time with my wife (their stepmother) and me, and her children have lived with us as well. My two children and my wife's two have developed a good relationship and enjoy spending time together.

My wife and I feel very fortunate to have been able to work out good relationships with all four children and with our former spouses. All four "children," now college-age, still live within twenty miles of us and we see them often. We are continually grateful for our good fortune, which has come with some luck and a lot of hard work. We have not escaped our share of problems, many of which are common to people in similar situations. Happily, one of these turned out to be a positive experience:

I remember one Christmas, when I was talking with my own children about how hard it must be for them to be torn between two families during a holiday. My daughter said, "Well, Dad, actually it has its advantages, too—we have two families we really like to be with, and besides, we get a lot more presents!" Of course, I liked that reply. She didn't say it to cheer me up, though; it was a statement about one of the several benefits of a stepfamily situation, and a confirmation that there is indeed a bright side to what could be viewed as a negative situation. Perhaps it also proves the point that it's not necessarily the situation but your outlook about it that really makes the difference.

While stepfamilies certainly have their advantages, they undeniably have some very real potential trouble spots as well. Not all stepfamilies experience them, but most do to some degree.

Everyone comes to a stepfamily life with some history of their own—both a personal history and a family history from their life "before." All the relationships and lifestyle components that made up each person's previous life don't just disappear when a new, blended family is formed. People may bring with them unfinished business about their other family, a divorce, feelings of self-doubt, guilt, anger, or fear about the future. Jealousy, competition, questions about money-handling, discipline or space may be especially powerful factors operating in the new family.

There are several important points to be made about stepfamilies and their unique situation and needs. First, there are two key words to keep in mind when thinking about stepfamilies: *complexity* and *preparation*.

Perhaps nowhere in American family life is there as much complexity as in stepfamilies. Because of this, careful preparation is called for to prepare people for their new lifestyle and to increase their chances of making it work out successfully. Such preparation can include not only careful thought and realistic planning, but also reading some of the many books and articles now available, going through counseling, participating in discussion or support groups, and talking to each other and other people.

I think a lack of realistic preparation for the complexities of the relationships and situations they will face is one of the major problems for new stepfamily members. Consider how someone's life changes when he enters into a new marriage and/or family. It involves many adjustments, especially if one or both of the new marriage partners have children. Then there are his parents and her parents, his ex-in-laws (his children's grandparents) and her ex-in-laws (her children's grandparents), his friends or former family friends, and hers, plus assorted other relatives, acquaintances, friends, and neighbors! That's quite a bit more complicated than the one set of family and friends in the traditional nuclear family, and it's a lot more difficult to handle.

Without realistic awareness and preparation, past histories and relationships can further complicate, and endanger, the new stepfamily. The following point about *roles* is related to this.

What are the roles played by each person in relation to people from the past and with each other now? If roles aren't clearly established, great stress can result. For instance, is the new husband called Dad or John by her children? Is the new wife called Mom or Mary by his children? Does the new spouse take a father-parent role, or is he "just" Mom's new husband, a friend for the children, but not a father figure? And how do ex-spouses fit in? What is their role as parents and how will their former-spouse status affect the new blended family? How do the children explain all this to their friends and deal with the feelings they have about it? Obviously, everyone's roles and identity shifts when there is a divorce or a change from being single to being married, especially when children are involved.

The most important advice in this chapter is: Take it slowly and avoid having too high expectations; be realistic instead.

This doesn't mean you should make no effort or avoid having any expectations at all, but rather that you should know positive changes are likely to take time, and lots of it. Trying to rush the process is more likely to endanger it than help it. It is realistic to expect that the average stepfamily will need anywhere from *one to five years* to establish clear and comfortable relationships, to understand and build the trust needed for smooth family roles to develop. No matter how much you want it, instant love and adjustment just does not happen, except in rare instances, and to expect it is to do everyone a great disservice. In time it will probably develop, but to force it invites disappointment, perhaps even resentment. Dr. Frederick Perls, a noted psychologist and psychiatrist, once said, "Don't push the river; it flows by itself."

At first, you can expect the children to accept your new spouse as an important person in their parent's life; perhaps they can see that person as their friend, and in time as a person for whom they have respect and love. But it will take time.

Another important piece of advice is: Remember the primary relationsip in any family, especially a stepfamily, is that of the husband and wife. After all, the stepfamily comes together because of their love and resulting relationship. Remembering this will be the key to staying clear about the focus of the stepfamily. This is not to negate the importance or place of children in a stepfamily; it is just to remind you of the main reason the stepfamily was formed in the first place. If couples can maintain a good understanding about their relationship and their importance to each other, they will be taking a giant step toward the whole family's stability and well-being. Without this kind of nurturing, the whole stepfamily is endangered, leaving the children without the anchor their parents' strong marriage can offer.

Consider carefully what the *rules* will be in the new family; how will they be established and by whom? Parents need to clarify their policies and wishes about such things as discipline, family structure and certain limits they may feel are important. How will you as parents resolve differences between yourselves on such matters as disciplinary practices? What if one parent in this blended family sees himself or herself as a parent and disciplinarian for the other spouse's children but the other parent sees this differently? This issue, if unresolved, can create major strains in the family. On the other hand, both parents may be clear about their roles and rules, but the children aren't happy about the situation. They might rather have their original parent back; they might see the newly united parents as a team to be divided and conquered if possible. The new parents must be secure enough to handle strains like this and help each other as well as the children handle the issues and feelings involved. If they are not, then even simple family chores can become big issues filled with confusion and resentment.

Parents don't have to be in full agreement, or start out with the same opinions about how situations should be handled, but they do have to work out a system for coping that will allow them to handle their family's issues well. This will likely involve compromise; it is important to develop a real united front, not a pretense.

Developing family rules can be especially difficult in a stepfamily in which there are children present from each partner's previous marriage. Jealousy, competition and the effects of each child's personal and family history can become important factors.

There may be some rules that will need to be developed between the parents themselves about such things as handling money, separate time with each parent's own children, or privacy. These are some of the issues that are often not anticipated but which can become sources of trouble if not anticipated and discussed. They may bring up feelings of jealousy or competition between the parents, who feel, "It's *my* money (child, time, or whatever)." Money can be a very emotional issue, particularly between people who may be used to handling it one way and find their new partner is used to handling it another way. Money-handling can be dealt with in many ways. Partners can pool the money; keep it separate; divide up family bills, each paying some out of their own earnings; treat income one way and other assets such as savings or investments another; and pay general family expenses out of pooled money but the expenses of one's children out of one's own income.

My experience is that handling money in the simplest possible way which satisfies each partner is best. Life is complicated enough without adding to its complexity any more than is necessary. One thing I suggest is that people discuss and decide what they prefer rather than making assumptions and then finding they have resentments about how the money situation turns out. My personal bias is to pool and share as much as possible, including children's expenses, because I think that encourages seeing the family's total welfare as both partners' responsibility. However, I know other stepfamilies that handle it differently and it works well for them.

As far as separate time with one's own children is concerned, I think it is a good idea as long as it is not seen as a way to isolate oneself from other family members. Rather, it should be a healthy continuation of the special relationship between a parent and child. I suggest that, if possible, each partner consider having some separate time with their stepchildren and that the parents together try to spend time with each of the children. However, there may not be enough hours in the day for all these good ideas. Each family has to do the best they can to work out these issues in ways that they feel will work well for them. Amidst all these relationships, the marriage partners must spend some time alone with each other, too.

Private time is important for most people but the amount and type of time varies widely. Hopefully, your family will allow you to have the time you feel you need, even if it is just ten minutes to glance at the newspaper after work or putter in the garage, kitchen, or yard. Women in our society often find it harder to find time to themselves because of an unspoken expectation that they will do the housework or cooking for the family. Husbands need to realize that their wives have the same need for time to themselves that they do; they should be willing to share family responsibilities. Of course, this is even more important if both partners work and are gone from home much of the day.

One more point regarding privacy—children need it too, probably more so in stepfamilies. This is particularly true in families where there are opposite sex stepchildren, and even more so if they are older and their sexuality is developing. Adolescent opposite sex stepchildren often experience some sexual attraction between each other, which is normal and even to be expected. Most handle this fine, either by avoiding each other when they are uncomfortable or by becoming good friends with clear boundaries. However, stepparents should be aware of this issue so any problems that may develop can be handled diplomatically before they get out of hand. One way parents can wisely intervene, even before intervention seems necessary, is to be sure appropriate rules exist about bathroom sharing, standards of dress/undress, and the amount of time children are alone together at home. In other words, be sure preventative measures are taken that will mean corrective measures are not needed later on.

Communication and respect for each individual's uniqueness and inherent value are very important. Dealing with the feelings, wishes and needs of each person can be an exceptionally difficult, complex task requiring great patience, skill, and dedication. You may need some short-term specialized professional help from someone familiar with and experienced in helping stepfamilies, or maybe this is the time to seek out a book on the subject, or to join a support group of other stepparents, or to make use of the potential benefits of family meetings, as discussed in Chapter 6.

A suggestion for stepfamilies which I think is a good one is to seriously consider moving from the homes each partner had before marriage to one that is "yours" after you become a new family. It is very difficult for many people to cope with feelings of territoriality when someone moves into "their" home, no matter how much you wish it were not so. I believe this is best handled by starting out together in a home that is new to everyone in the family, even if this means a place that is a step down from the one you could have shared by moving into one of the partner's existing homes. This is a relatively small price to pay to avoid a potentially destructive conflict. Not all people will need to take this step, but it is something worthy of an honest discussion.

To summarize: (1) Remember to respect the uniqueness of being a stepparent; (2) keep in mind the two key concepts for stepfamilies: complexity and (the need for) preparation; (3) be aware of the multiple roles involved in a stepfamily, for both children and parents; (4) be prepared to cope with the related issues regarding slowly developing relationships and the danger of expectations that are too high; (5) develop family rules that will meet the varied needs of everyone in your complex stepfamily arrangement; (6) finally, consider the possibility of starting out in your new life together with a home that is "yours" rather than "his" or "hers" as a way of respecting the potential impact of family members' histories and expressing your commitment to your marriage and new family.

Most stepfamilies are born in the shadow of some kind of loss. Yet they represent an exciting new beginning, an opportunity to put into practice some of the lessons learned in life. In every way you can, give yourself and your family the best possible chance for success in your new adventure together.

CHAPTER 9
LIVING WITH YOUR TEENAGER
Understanding Them And You

On the way to my office one day recently, I stopped at several medical offices and schools to leave information on two workshops I would be teaching the following month, one intended for parents of teenagers and one for parents under stress. At two of the stops, the receptionists read the flyers describing the workshops and said something like, "Oh, boy, I sure could use both of these! I've got teenagers myself and I'm ready to throw in the towel about four out of seven days of the week lately."

At another office, a teacher and office secretary were present and commented on the title of the workshop for parents, ("Living Successfully With Your Teenager"), saying, "Do you think it can be done?" They then laughed self-consciously, but the concern behind the comment was obviously serious.

I think it *is* possible to live successfully with your teenager, but if you listen to the complaints and concerns and consternation of the parents of teens, you might think otherwise.

When someone asks me what I think about the teen years, I often say, "Well, I think the task of the adolescent is mainly to survive to age twenty in one piece; the task of their parents is to hang on 'til adolescence is over!"

A more serious, accurate answer to the question of what the teen years are all about is that adolescence, as a stage in life, is the time when teenagers put together an "act" that works in the world, and when they develop who they really are.

Put even more briefly, the teen years mean one thing:

change (or transition). The task of this particular period of child-hood development, which I consider to be the period between ages twelve and twenty, is simply to change from being a child to being an adult. But it certainly isn't as simple a task as that statement indicates on the surface.

It is a monumental task to accomplish in just a few years—changing from being a child to a fully functioning adult, with no prior experience and few inherent guidelines. It is a time when the body changes drastically; hormonal changes bring about physical and emotional change which the child is completely unfamiliar with; urges about sexuality emerge; there are peer pressures to behave or not behave in certain ways; and other new opportunities and temptations of all kinds present themselves in abundance. Even the structure of school, which up to now has been one of the constants in the child's life, is changing. The new adolescent goes from the one-class-all-day of grade school to the multiple classes and teachers of intermediate and high school. There are growing pressures to choose the right subjects, get good grades (his or her future depends on it) and choose a career. Accomplishing these tasks consistently, competently and comfortably is no small chore for this child-adult. It's a lot for a young teenager to have to deal with well, even if he or she really wants to do well in school and knows what career to choose.

Not infrequently, there are changes taking place in the family as well, as the child is busy becoming an adult. After twelve to twenty years of marriage, many adults are entering mid-life, with its potential problems. They may be changing careers as they adjust to the halfway mark in life, or they may even be changing spouses—not exactly an event to inspire security and serenity for the adolescent. This is a time when parents are likely to become aware they are not getting any younger. Perhaps they feel they are financially unprepared for their future retirement, or feel they have missed out on the career advancements they wanted or the recognition they deserved. They may feel physically or sexually under par, or socially unsuccessful. Such events in a parent's life certainly can have an effect on the whole family's condition. It is an interesting quirk of nature that it is possible for both adolescents and parents to go through potentially difficult and important changes at about the same time in their lives.

I'd like to suggest you now take a few minutes to look at some of your own opinions and feelings about teenagers and about being a parent of teens. First, think for a moment about this question: What do you think are the main problems of adolescence; what things would you list as concerns you or other parents of teens have for their teenagers?

When I ask this question in my workshop for parents of teens, a very long list usually results. Typically, this list includes the following comments about teenagers: They seem to lack respect; are very independent; are tempermental, brooding, moody, and overly emotional; are often lazy, careless, even slovenly; are very impressionable; are shortsighted; care about their friends too much (more than about the family); are sneaky, secretive, belligerent, critical, impatient, demanding; idealistic, self-conscious, and insecure; have messy rooms; dress carelessly and/or outrageously; often test limits and defy discipline; can be easily bored; don't care enough about school; won't communicate; don't take responsibility for themselves enough; like strange music; won't come home on time; and are often hungry! Almost always, the terrible trio of sex/drugs/alcohol is mentioned as the most scary aspect of the teen years.

That's quite a list of problems and concerns, but it is one that most parents of adolescents can relate to, at least in part. The adolescent years are indeed times of stress, change, growth, experimentation, and struggle for teenagers and their parents.

Now I would like you to take a moment to think about, and list on a piece of paper, anything that comes to mind in response to this question: What was life like for *you* as a teenager? And how many "teenage attributes" in the above list do you feel were true of you to some degree during those years? Take a few minutes to honestly reflect on this.

Next, ask yourself this question: How is teen life today different than it was for your generation? Most people agree it is different In many ways, such as: teenagers today have more mobility and more options or choices because of the way life is today; more teens have cars; there are more things to do now than were available to most of us about twenty years ago; and there is generally more of a sense of independence than we experienced. There is certainly more influence on our lives from the media today—television, movies, video games, radio—and there is a much greater variety of magazines and other reading material. There are different societal standards regarding sex, and drugs and other temptations are more available. There is more freedom and less authority at school. LIfe is lived at a faster pace and is generally more complex today than it was for parents who were teens twenty years ago. Finally, we did not worry nearly as much about "The Bomb" and the tenuousness of life as many, many teenagers do today; you might be surprised how often I hear teens express concern about this fearsome issue and the possibility that they may not live to age forty because of it.

These complications do not provide an excuse for teens to "get off the hook" for their behavior. However, when added to the already rather overwhelming tasks that a teen must undertake as he or she makes the transition from childhood to adulthood, they make this an even more difficult time.

A family I worked with is an example of some of the problems the teen years can cause. Bob and Betty Jackson and their two children, Cindy and Bob, Jr., had been struggling with their family's problems for some time. At the time I started seeing them, Cindy was fourteen and Bob, Jr., was almost sixteen. Family arguments had become so intense that both children's schoolwork had been affected and the school's assistant principal finally called in Bob and Betty to discuss the kids' falling grades. It became obvious during their discussion that there was a great deal of tension between the parents and between them and their children, so it was suggested the family go for some short-term counseling to try to sort out the problems before they got worse.

As I talked with Bob and Betty at our first appointment, they could hardly contain their anger at feeling betrayed by their children's actions. They were afraid that they would end up losing all control over them. Cindy was becoming increasingly belligerent and uncommunicative, and Bob, Jr. was hanging out with less-than-desirable friends. Both were on the verge of flunking at least one class and seemed not to care about how their lives were going.

I saw Cindy alone for half of the next appointment and Bob, Jr. for the other half, then saw them together the next week. The two had a fairly close relationship, at least close enough that they felt they could talk with me together and share some of their views on the family's situation. Both felt their parents loved them but were being over-protective, and the children felt smothered. They felt they couldn't do what they wanted without receiving intense questioning almost daily. A power struggle had developed and no one in the family was handling it satisfactorily.

Bob and Betty, like so many parents today, both worked and were under stress from their jobs and the struggle to offer their family the best life they could. They worried constantly about the influences on their children at school and elsewhere. Bob and Betty felt the best way to protect them was to keep tabs on their lives as much as possible, offering advice, love and guidance. Unfortunately, Cindy and Bob, Jr. felt their parents didn't trust them; that they just wanted them to stay at home most of the time and not have the friends they wanted or pursue the things that interested them, including some rather unusual music and clothes.

When I saw the family together—not an easy task since they weren't sure they could even be in the same room without a big scene occurring—we talked about each person's feelings about him or herself and the family as a unit. It became clear that they had had trouble communicating for a long time. Each harbored his own fears and preconceived ideas about what the others thought. The parents were trying to guide their children as best they could, while Cindy and Bob, Jr. felt they could best stay out of trouble at home by avoiding their parents whenever possible. The result was that no one felt satisfied and fears and resentment grew as time went by. Much of Cindy and Bob, Jr.'s school and other problems were the result of them acting out behaviors which were intended—largely unconsciously—to show their independence, and, surprisingly, to get attention from their parents. In part, they were saying, "We know things aren't going very well, but this is the only way we know of to handle our lives and to ask for help."

It was fortunate that the school personnel were alert and caring enough to step forward and intervene tactfully. After more discussions about everyone's feelings and opinions, all four members of the family became more understanding, tolerant and compromising, without feeling they had given in more than was comfortable for them. More open communication developed and appropriate, effective family rules resulted in place of the game-playing and avoidance that had characterized their family life previously. Of course, tense times still occurred sometimes, but they were much better able to handle crises with their new attitudes and tools. They developed a growing sense of trust and understanding of each other's needs.

Often it seems that teenagers are becoming "bad" especially if they are "acting out" a lot, and parents react to this with fear and panic, and perhaps feel betrayed. This scenario is likely to occur for most families at some time during adolescence.

It is usual—even normal—for teenagers to try different things in their search for themselves. Many go through stages of experimenting with styles of hair, clothes, and music, different kinds of friends and leisure activities, displaying posters on their bedroom walls or dumping piles of dirty clothes on the floor, seeking changes in their curfew hours, or finding out how much beer they can drink or pot they can smoke without being detected when they get home. Some of these adolescent experiments can be not just perplexing to their parents, but may be dangerous. It is at these times that a parent's skill at communication, effective response and realistic rule-setting can be tested to the limits.

What is usually happening at these times is not that the teenager is becoming really "bad", at least not intentionally, but that he or she is seeking to establish an identity in this period of uncertainty and confusion. The teen is testing limits to see what they really are, perhaps testing or examining the values of parents or society, trying to find out how the world works and whether he can handle life effectively. In this time of search, evaluation and trial and error, teens need their parents to be deeply caring, understanding, yet firm, intervening with more wisdom than emotion.

The "badness" we see may really just be a teenager's sometimes clumsy attempts to be different, to be "himself". Or it may be acting out—behaving negatively or destructively. The latter is usually a statement of some kind, perhaps of dissatisfaction, unhappiness or discontent. It often happens when a message is not getting through by other means; it is actually a form of communication. The wise parent or teacher looks beneath the obvious for hidden messages, however scary, unpleasant or confusing they may be.

Remember, adolescents are really growing-up children struggling to become adults without any prior experience of how to do this well. They are trying to put together their "act" for the world, not yet knowing that the best act is just being themselves. It's not easy being the parent who loves them and has to watch this agonizing process.

Successful relationships are among the most difficult things to have in life, especially close and lasting ones. A successful relationship with a developing teen is particularly hard to have work out well, at least consistently. Don't expect too much of either yourself or your teen or you will be disappointed. Just expect all you realistically can, so each of you will be challenged and will keep moving ahead.

Keep in mind that your loyalty to each other is most important and don't let individual events or temporary setbacks throw you off course. Stay clear about your love and caring during disagreements or times of crisis. Don't allow yourselves to violate or destroy your deeper, lasting feelings just because you are momentarily alienated or afraid. Try to *respond* wisely to situations rather than *react* to them out of sheer emotion. Avoid the temptation to say or do things that will tear down the other person's self-esteem in a moment of anger; deal carefully and honestly with the anger instead. It is probably fueled by *temporary* hurt, fear or feelings of hate.

With teenagers, perhaps more than any other age, several parenting skills are important. One is to remember what love is: caring about a person as he is now, and having a commitment to his well-being. Another is the importance of self-image and self-esteem; self-image being one's identity as a person and self-esteem being the evaluation of self-image—high or low, good or bad, positive or negative, better or worse than others, desirable or unacceptable.

Two very significant parenting skills we discussed earlier are rules and discipline, and communication. Parental discipline was defined as being "training for self-discipline." Communication, the most vital ingredient in a relationship, the very foundation of a good one, is the means through which we connect with another person, the way we share and get to know each other. Keep these skills in mind, especially when your children are in the transition between childhood and adulthood.

One of the things that's often hard about having children grow up is that your role as a parent changes as they get older. As young children, they needed constant care, clear and specific rules and limits, close supervision and were generally very dependent on you. You had a great deal of influence and authority in their lives. But as they grow and become individuals in their own right, more autonomous and independent, the roles and the balance between children and parents changes. For older teens and young adults, the parental role becomes less that of an authority figure and more that of the "invited guest" in their lives.

During these years it becomes important to begin letting go of our expectations and regrets, of our old images of our children and ourselves, and learn to deal with who they, and we, really are now. This can be the foundation of a new kind of relationship that is both more appropriate and more healthy, for both parents and their children.

Letting go of the past, shifting gears and getting on with the realities of life may sound easy, but it's often hard to do. This may be the time for a new beginning for *parents*, though it may be hard to see at first, when they reevaluate themselves as individuals or as a couple and find new ways to enrich their lives, clarify their own identity and move on to a new level of satisfaction and purpose in life.

SECTION IV
THERE'S STILL TIME

CHAPTER 10
THE MOST IMPORTANT ADVICE FOR PARENTS
Remember To . . .

In this last, brief chapter, I'd like to share with you the "Closing Statement" which I offer people in my workshops on parenting. I hope it will summarize for you all I've tried to say:

People sometimes ask me: What is the most important advice you can offer parents, briefly stated?

My answer is this: Learn the few basic parenting techniques we all need to know, then remember to:

- Give yourself credit for what you've done right, and trust that you children will turn out well, even if you did make a few mistakes. Be willing to see mistakes as learning experiences, not awful events.

- Realize that you and your children are doing the best you can at any given time, even if there is room for improvement. It's kinder to look for progress than for perfection.

- Talk to your children. Build a relationship rather than just waiting for them to grow up. Take time together, relax and enjoy each other whenever you can. Yet give them room to grow, to be themselves, to make decisions, even to make some mistakes.

- Look at parenting as helping your children become more fully who they are, and trust that this is good. Be aware that it is your support, love, and guidance that opens the way for their growth and fulfillment, to their becoming the best person they can possibly be. Look at it as being the president of their fan club!

- Take good care of yourself—you need and deserve this and it is also a gift to those who love you. Meet your own needs for nurturing relationships, healthy self-esteem, and effective communication. Add to this whatever else is necessary to make you a better person and a happier parent.

Finally, ask yourself this question: Even though my children and I have sometimes had problems, will I be glad when they are grown that I handled things the way I did?

If the answer is yes, be grateful. But if it is no, start now to do whatever you can to make changes so that the answer can become yes.

Don't give up. There is still time.

ADDENDUM
Some Reading Suggestions

SOME READING SUGGESTIONS

GENERAL INTEREST

Dinkmeyer, Don and Gary McKay, *The Parents Handbook: Systematic Training For Effective Parenting*. Circle Pines: American Guidance Service, 1982. (This book and *S.T.E.P./ Teen* by the same authors are excellent on a number of subjects of interest to parents.)

Dobson, James, *The Strong-Willed Child*. Wheaton: Tyndale House, 1978.

Dodson, Fitzhugh, *How To Parent*. New York: New American Library, 1973.

Emery, Stewart, *Actualizations: You Don't Have To Rehearse To Be Yourself*. Garden City: Dolphin Books, Doubleday & Co., Inc., 1978. (Thought-provoking reading regarding parental philosophy and roles and basic issues such as communication.)

Gordon, Thomas, *Parent Effectiveness Training*. New York: Peter H. Wyden, Inc., 1970.

Gordon, Thomas, *P.E.T. In Action*. New York: Bantam Books, 1976.

Ilg, Ames and Baker, *Child Behavior* (Revised Edition). New York: Harper & Row, 1981. (Good general developmental information.)

Kiley, Dan, *Keeping Kids Out Of Trouble*. New York: Warner Books, 1978.

Kiley, Dan, *Keeping Parents Out Of Trouble*. New York: Warner Books, 1982.

Lerman, Saf, *Parent Awareness Training: Positive Parenting For The 1980s*. New York: A & W Publishing, Inc., 1980.

Osman, Betty, *Learning Disabilities: A Family Affair*. New York: Random House, Inc., 1979.

Rogers, Florence, *Parenting The Difficult Child*. Radnor: Chilton Book Co., 1979.
Rogers, Fred and Barry Head, *Mr. Rogers Talks With Parents*. New York: Berkley Books, 1983. (Recent book by star of the television show "Mr. Rogers' Neighborhood.")
Satir, Virginia, *Peoplemaking*. Palo Alto: Science & Behavior Books, 1972.

PARENTAL STRESS AND BURNOUT

Eliot, Dr. Robert S. and Dennis Breo, *Is It Worth Dying For?: A Self-Assessment Program To Make Stress Work For You, Not Against You*. New York: Bantam Books, 1984.
Freudenberger, Herbert, *Burn-Out: How To Beat The High Cost of Success*. New York: Bantam Books, 1980. (Burnout as it relates to many aspects of life.)
Jaffe, Dennis T. and Cynthia D. Scott, *From Burnout To Balance: A Workbook For Personal Self-Renewal*. New York: McGraw Hill, 1984.
Procaccini, Joseph and Mark Kiefaber, *Parent Burnout*. New York: Signet Books, New American Library, 1983.
Sher, Barbara, *Wishcraft: How To Get What You Really Want*. New York: Ballantine Books, Inc., 1983.

SELF-IMAGE/SELF-ESTEEM

Borba, Michele and Craig Borba, *Self-Esteem: A Classroom Affair*. Minneapolis: Winston Press, 1978.
Briggs, Dorothy Corkille, *Your Child's Self-Esteem*. Garden City: Dolphin Books, Doubleday & Co., Inc., 1975. (An excellent book with information on each stage of growth and development, on power/authority/discipline as related issues, as well as on self-esteem and its importance.)
Carothers, James and Ruth Gasten, *Helping Children To Like Themselves: Activities For Building Self-Esteem*. Livermore: RJ Associates, 1978.
Clarke, Jean Illsley, *Self-Esteem: A Family Affair*. Minneapolis: Winston Press, Inc., 1978. (Discusses self-esteem as it relates to family life at each age, and stage of development.)

Clarke, Clemes and Bean, *How To Raise Teenagers' Self-Esteem*. San Jose: Enrich, Division of OHAUS, 1980.

Clemes, Harris and Reynold Bean, *Self-Esteem: The Key To Your Child's Well-Being*. New York: Putnam Publishing Group, 1981.

Cline, Victor, *How To Make Your Child A Winner: Ten Keys To Rearing Successful Children*. New York: Walker & Co., 1980.

RULES AND DISCIPLINE

Bodenhamer, Gregory, *Back In Control*. Englewood Cliffs: Prentice-Hall, 1983.

Canter, Lee with Marlene Canter, *Assertive Discipline: A Take Charge Approach For Today's Educator*. Los Angeles: Canter & Associates, Inc., 1976.

Canter, Lee with Marlene Canter, *Assertive Discipline For Parents*. Los Angeles: Canter & Associates, Inc., 1982.

Dobson, James, *Dare To Discipline*. Wheaton: Tyndale House Publishing, 1970.

Dodson, Fitzhugh, *How To Discipline With Love*. New York: Signet Books, New American Library, 1978.

Dreikurs, Rudolph and Loren Gray, *A Parent's Guide To Child Discipline*. New York: E. P. Dutton, 1970.

Dreikurs, Rudolph and Loren Gray, *A New Approach To Discipline: Logical Consequences*. New York: E. P. Dutton, 1968.

Wood, Paul and Bernard Schwartz, *How To Get Your Children To Do What You Want Them To Do*. Englewood Cliffs: Prentice-Hall, Inc., 1977. (Very good on effective demands as part of discipline.)

SINGLE AND/OR WORKING PARENTS

Ashery, Rebecca and Michele Basen, *The Parents With Careers Workbook*. Washington, D.C.: Acropolis Books, 1983.

Duncan, Barbara, *The Single Mother's Survival Manual*, Saratoga, California: R & E Publishers, 1984.

Greywolf, Elizabeth S., *The Single Mother's Handbook*. New

York: Wm. Morrow & Co., 1984.

Hope, Karol and Nancy Young, *Momma, The Sourcebook For Single Mothers*. New York: New American Library, 1976.

Klein, Carole, *The Single Parent Experience*. New York: Avon Books, 1978.

Long, Lynette and Thomas Long, *The Handbook For Latchkey Children & Their Parents*. New York: Arbor House Publishing Co., 1983.

Norris, Gloria and JoAnn Miller, *The Working Mother's Complete Handbook*. (Revised) New York: New American Library, 1979 and 1984.

DIVORCE AND RELATED ISSUES

Galper, Miriam, *Joint Custody and Co-Parenting: Sharing Your Child Equally*. Philadelphia: Running Press, 1980.

Gardner, Richard, *The Parents Book About Divorce; The Boys and Girls Book About Divorce; The Boys and Girls Book About One-Parent Familes; The Boys and Girls Book About Stepfamilies*. New York: Bantam Books, 1977, 1970, 1983, 1982.

Richards, Arlene and Irene Willis, *How To Get It Together When Your Parents Are Coming Apart*. New York: Bantam Books, 1977.

Salk, Lee, *What Every Child Would Like His Parents To Know About Divorce*. New York: Warner Books, 1978.

Ware, Ciji, *Sharing Parenthood After Divorce*. New York: The Viking Press, 1982.

CHILD/ADOLESCENT DEVELOPMENT AND SELF-HELP BOOKS

Bell, Ruth, et.al., *Changing Bodies, Changing Lives: A Book For Teens on Sex and Relationships*. New York: Random House, 1980.

Berman, Claire, *What Am I Doing In A Stepfamily?* Secaucus: Lyle Stuart, Inc., 1982.

Dobson, James, *Preparing For Adolescence*. New York: Bantam Books, 1980. (For parents and teens, with a Christian viewpoint.)

Freed, Alvyn, *TA For Teens (And Other Important People)*. Rolling Hills Estate: Jalmar Press, 1976. (Information and self-help exercises.)

Gordon, Sol, *The Teenage Survival Book*. New York: Times Books, 1981.

Livingston, Carole, *Why Was I Adopted?* Secaucus: Lyle Stuart, Inc., 1978.

Mayle, Peter, *What's Happening To Me?* Secaucus: Lyle Stuart, Inc., 1975. (About changes, puberty, related issues for early teens.)

McCoy, Kathy and Charles Wibbelsman, M.D., *The Teenage Body Book*. New York: Wallaby Books (Simon & Schuster), 1978 and 1984.

Robson, Bonnie, *My Parents Are Divorced, Too: Teenagers Talk About Their Experiences and How They Cope*. New York: Dodd, Mead & Co., 1980.

The Boston Women's Health Book Collective, *Ourselves and Our Children: A Book By and For Parents*. New York: Random House, 1978.

FOR FATHERS

Dodson, Fitzhugh, *How To Father*. New York: New American Library, 1975.

Shechtman, Stephen and Wenda G. Singer, *Real Men Enjoy Their Kids: How To Spend Quality Time With The Children In Your Life*. Nashville: Abingdon Press, 1983.

Sullivan, S. Adams, *The Fathers Almanac*. Garden City: Doubleday & Co., 1980.

Yablonsky, Lewis, *Fathers and Sons*. Austin: S & S Press, 1982. (Good for fathers and/or sons of any age.)

STEPPARENTING

Berman, Claire, *Making It As a Stepparent*. New York: Bantam Books, 1981. (Discusses a wide variety of issues facing stepfamilies.)

Einstein, Elizabeth, *The Stepfamily: Living, Loving & Learning*.

New York: Macmillan, 1982.

Maddox, Brenda, *The Half-Parent: Living With Other People's Children*. New York: M. Evans & Co., Inc., 1975.

Noble, June and William Noble, *How To Live With Other People's Children*. New York: E. P. Dutton, 1979.

Roosevelt, Ruth and Jeannette Lofas, *Living In Step: A Remarriage Manual For Parents and Children*. New York: McGraw Hill, 1977. (Discusses unique position and role of each family member.)

Rosenbaum, Jean and Veryl, *Stepparenting*. New York: E. P. Dutton, 1978. (Written by a husband and wife who are both psychotherapists and are both stepchildren and stepparents.)

Visher, Emily and John Visher, *How To Win As A Stepfamily*. Chicago: Contemporary Books, Inc., 1983.

Visher, Emily and John Visher, *Stepfamilies: A Guide To Working With Stepparents and Stepchildren*. Secaucus: The Citadel Press, 1980. (Also written by a husband and wife who are psychotherapists and stepparents.)

TEENAGERS AND THE ADOLESCENT YEARS

Anderson, Joan Webster, *Teen Is A Four-Letter Word*. White Hall: Betterway Publications, Inc., 1983.

Bayard, Robert and Jean, *How To Deal With Your Acting-Up Teenager*. New York: M. Evans & Co., Inc., 1981. (A comprehensive, step-by-step program.)

Bell, Ruth and Leni Zeiger Wildflower, *Talking With Your Teenager: A Book For Parents*. New York: Random House, 1983.

Buntman, Peter and Eleanor Saris, *How To Live With Your Teenager: A Survivor's Handbook For Parents*. Pasadena: The Birch Tree Press, 1979.

Dinkmeyer, Don and Gary McKay, *The Parent's Guide: Systematic Training For Effective Parenting Of Teens*. Circle Pines: American Guidance Service, 1983.

Fishman, Meryl and Kathleen Horwich, *Living With Your Teenage Daughter and Liking It*. Austin: S & S Press, 1983.

Ginott, Haim, *Between Parent and Child; Between Parent and Teenager*. New York: Avon Books, 1965, 1969.

McCoy, Kathleen, *Coping With Teenage Depression: A Parent's*

Guide. New York: New American Library, 1982.

Paine, Roger W., *We Never Had Any Trouble Before: First Aid For Parents Of Teenagers*. Briarcliff Manor: Stein & Day, 1975.

Rosenbaum, Jean and Veryl, *Living With Teenagers*. Briarcliffe Manor: Stein & Day, 1980. (Detailed information, good guidance.)

Schowalter, John E. and Walter R. Anyan, *The Family Handbook of Adolescence: A Comprehensive, Medically Oriented Guide To The Years From Puberty To Adulthood*. New York: Alfred A. Knopf, Inc., 1979.

Winship, Elizabeth, *Reaching Your Teenager*. Boston: Houghton Mifflin Co., 1983. (Written by newspaper columnist "Ask Beth.")

Note: This list is not intended to be exhaustive, nor is it an endorsement of any book. It is just a partial list of what is available. If you have comments, or suggestions for books to be added in future editions, please contact me:

Dennis Lees, Ph.D.
1700 Ygnacio Valley Road, Suite 200
Walnut Creek, California 94598
Telephone: (415) 935-4256